D0900369

*The Psychology
of Behavior Exchange*

The Psychology
of Behavior Exchange

KENNETH J. GERGEN
Swarthmore College

ADDISON-WESLEY PUBLISHING COMPANY
Reading, Massachusetts
Menlo Park, California • *London* • *Don Mills, Ontario*

TOPICS IN SOCIAL PSYCHOLOGY
Charles A. Kiesler, Yale University, Series Editor

*To lessons learned in the
Clipper Ship*

Foreword

It is becoming increasingly difficult for anyone to be a generalist in social psychology. Not only is the number of articles published zooming, but new researchable areas of interest are multiplying as well. A researcher finds more fascinating topics these days than he used to, but he also finds himself behind in his reading of all but one or two of them. As a result, the quality of the broad introductory book in social psychology has suffered. No one can any longer be an expert in all of social psychology.

As an alternative, we offer the present series, *Topics in Social Psychology,* directed toward the student with no prior background in social psychology. Taken as a whole, the series adequately covers the field of social psychology, but it has the advantage that each short book was written by an expert in the area. The instructor can select some subset of the books to make up his course, the particular subset depending on his biases and inclinations. In addition, the individual volumes can be useful in several ways: as supplementary readings in, perhaps, a sociology course; to introduce more advanced courses (for example, a graduate seminar in attitude change); or just for peeking at recent developments in social psychology.

In this volume, Kenneth Gergen has focused on an exciting and relatively new topic in social psychology—exchange theory. The issues involved are broad and cross disciplinary lines. Gergen has done an excellent job of bringing these diverse elements together, while at the same time showing the reader some of the excitement of tracking a research question down.

Charles A. Kiesler

Contents

The Psychology
of Behavior Exchange

CHAPTER ONE

Toward an Adequate Theory

Most psychologists share with their students, at least privately, certain dis-satisfactions with the progress that the field of psychology has made thus far. On the one hand, there are the cold abstractions developed in the experimental laboratory, abstractions that so nicely account for the behavior of animals, but somehow fail to capture the essence of everyday life on the human level. On the other hand, there are the grand theorists, such as Freud, who burrow headlong into the intimacies of human relations, only to develop sweeping generalizations without support in fact. And one complaint that is often leveled against both the "hard" and the "soft" brands of psychology is that they are burdened by excessive terminology. The impolite way of saying it is that psychologists are full of jargon. Now the psychologist's shin is just as thin as anyone else's, and each of these criticisms presents a challenge. No psychologist wishes to see his major contribution to knowledge deposited on the slag heap of empty words.

This volume will allow you to experience at first hand the process of developing a theory of human interaction. We shall take a close look at theoretical terms, and ask ourselves whether or not we need them—what uses they serve. We shall examine factual data, trying to ascertain their implications for theory. We shall confront the methods of the experimental social psychologist, methods that are avowed to be the most rigorous and scientifically valid of those yet developed. We shall face up to some of the knotty problems that have long caused the psychologist's life to be a restless one. And, to be sure, in the process of developing a theory we are doomed to make mistakes. Hopefully, we can remain aware of our errors, in order that one day the special insight, the needed fact, or the auspicious turn in methodology may allow us to advance that much further.

But we shall not make this journey in solitude, cut away from historical precedent and accumulated wisdom. On the contrary, we shall lean heavily on a tradition in the making. It is often difficult to pinpoint the time and place at which a "school of thought" or an "intellectual tradition" develops and becomes recognized as an entity. However, at the writing of this book, we are in the midst of developing a unified orientation to understanding social behavior: the orientation that has often been characterized by the term "behavior exchange." It is one that places a high premium on facts gathered through experimentation. Within the orientation concepts tend to be developed inductively, springing from quantifiable data rather than from fantasy or supposition. This orientation remains cognizant of developments in the animal laboratory, and yet remains open to the specialized problems that emerge when human beings interact. The view of man is not flattering: he is seen as basically motivated for his own ends, utilizing all cognitive and behavioral means at his disposal to achieve these ends in a complex world.

Major contributors to the psychology of behavior exchange have included Peter Blau, Morton Deutsch, Erving Goffman, George Homans, Edward E. Jones, Harold Kelley, Anatol Rapoport, and John Thibaut, to name but a few. The names mean little at this stage, and a brief volume such as this can do no more than introduce several of the core ideas. The bibliographies at the end of each chapter are to invite the reader to probe more deeply.

One important historical legacy deserves our attention at the very outset. In building a theory of social behavior, we must know something about the process of theory construction. What, after all, makes one theory better than another? Why isn't one man's opinion as good as the next? Philosophers as well as psychologists have given this question a good deal of thought, and if we are to do a decent job with our theory building, the major issues should be brought into the open.

CRITERIA FOR THEORY CONSTRUCTION

Let us begin with a concrete question. College students often find that they disagree sharply with those outside the college environment—particularly if the latter are over 30, and more often than not, if they happen to be parents. Research has also shown that values and attitudes within a group tend to become more homogeneous over time. Thus, a college student will tend to develop values that are common within the college population. These values are often different from those found in, let us say, the middle-class, middle-aged population. However, we must proceed to the question: What happens to a person's values as he moves from one group to another? College students do not always remain at college. They may spend their vacations at home and reside there for the summer. In such situations their views may be alien to those around them. The specific question, then, is: What changes occur in a student's values as a result of his sojourn in an alien culture? Would you expect his values to change? If so, in what direction—toward the values in the home environment or away? And most important, for what reason would you expect the change to occur? What is your *theory?*

As it happens, there are data relevant to this issue. Philip Brickman, while a senior honors student at Harvard, explored the problem in the following way. Some weeks prior to Christmas vacation some 72 undergraduates filled out two questionnaires. Both of the questionnaires dealt with values. Standardized items explored the students' feelings about such issues as obeying authority, sensuality, equality, and the manipulation of other people. The second questionnaire asked about the students' perceptions of the norms both at Harvard and at home. The student thus indicated what he felt to be the norm at Harvard on each of the dimensions, as well as the norm in his home environment. When the students returned from spending some three weeks at home over Christmas, they were again asked to fill out a questionnaire—a repeat of the initial measure exploring their own values.

The data analysis was confined to those items in which the following configuration occurred in the *initial* testing period: the student's perception of the Harvard norm fell to one side of his own value, and the perceived home norm to the other. In the following example we see a 10-point scale for one of the items concerning social equality:

Poverty could be almost entirely done away with if we made certain basic changes in our social and economic system.

	Disagree								Agree	
Own View:	−5	−4	−3	−2	−1	(+1)	+2	+3	+4	+5
Harvard Norm:	−5	−4	−3	−2	−1	+1	+2	+3	(+4)	+5
Home Norm:	−5	(−4)	−3	−2	−1	+1	+2	+3	+4	+5

As you can see, the student perceives the Harvard environment as being extremely liberal (as most students did), while his own value is not quite so liberal (as most weren't) and the view he saw most prevalent at home was on the conservative end of the continuum (with generally high agreement). In effect, Brickman confined his analysis to cases of maximal conflict—where the students' values fell somewhere between the polarities represented by the two reference groups. In concrete terms, the focus of the study was on whether the students' value ratings would move toward the perceived home or perceived Harvard norm as a result of their having spent several weeks in the former environment. Perhaps by now you have formulated your own prediction about what Brickman was to find, and a supporting rationale for the prediction.

It is with the question of rationale that we can return to the original issue: What makes one theory or rationale better than another? What criteria can be used to compare theories? Using the study of student values as a point of departure, we list the following criteria as most important to consider:

1. Predictive capability. The most elementary criterion that may be brought to bear is whether one's reasoning, or theory building, leads him to a correct prediction or not. For example, the Marxian theory of class struggle and the inevitable emergence of a classless society may account nicely for events in a number of cultures. In the main, however, it has failed to predict the course of history for most countries, and thus it does not in this respect constitute a "good" theory.

But what about student values? What did your reasoning lead you to predict? Brickman reasoned that if a person was a member of one reference group (e.g., college) and moved for a short period into an alien reference group (home), those in the latter group would react to him primarily as a member of the former. Thus, the family and friends of the student would generally behave toward him as if he held the views prevailing at college. In questioning or discussing the values held in the college community, he would be called upon to defend the college norm by virtue of his membership in that community. He would thus be forced to *play the role* of the typical student at his college, with the net effect that he would become even more committed to the values he felt to be normative at his college. He would think of reasons to support these values, search for criticisms of potential opponents, and, over time, convince himself. His values would not change toward those of his friends and family, but on the contrary, would move toward the perceived college norm.

Did this reasoning lead to an accurate prediction? As it turned out, student values did undergo a statistically significant shift in the direction of the perceived college norm. College students essentially became *more* collegiate as a result of spending time away from college. In terms of predictive capability, the theory proved to be a good one.

Now it is also quite likely that some readers have made the opposite prediction. After all, you know of situations in which a person has moved from one reference group to another and has simply shed the skin of his older existence. If this were not so, immigrants would never be assimilated into society and incoming freshmen at a college would never shed their homespun values for those they stumble upon in college (and later shed again). And it does make sense that the attempt of people to please others and to be liked by them usually brings them into closer agreement. This appears to be perfectly valid reasoning. Should we, because this reasoning did not predict in the present case, jettison this latter approach altogether?

No, what we can do is search for characteristics that distinguish between the case of the college student going home and that of the immigrant or incoming freshman. Such distinctions may ultimately be used to expand and enrich the theory. For example, one difference between the student going home and the immigrant is that the former is not seeking to establish membership in the alien culture, whereas the latter is. Another difference is that the freshman and the immigrant are spending a far greater period of time in the new culture. Perhaps under such conditions as these, the opposite of Brickman's results would be expected. In fact, Brickman's data showed that students who spent the greatest amount of time at home during the vacation were least likely to move toward the Harvard norm. By drawing these distinctions and examining relevant data, we have managed to expand the theory in important ways and to further the predictive capabilities of the theory.

2. Linkage with observables. Theories are by nature stated in abstract terms. To be sure, some theories are more abstract than others. To say that frustration leads to aggression is a broad, inclusive, and highly general theoretical statement. It is much more abstract than a theory about what your brother will do when he finds his bicycle is stolen. But regardless of level of abstraction or generality, theoretical terms may also differ in another very important way: the extent to which they can be linked to observable entities. We can point to many examples of aggression, and also agree on what the terms "reference group" and "norms" refer to in the Brickman study of students' values. On the other hand, if we had used concepts such as "will" or "soul," we might have had a very difficult time in specifying observable referents.

The degree of linkage between abstract terms and real-world entities is of cardinal significance when one wishes to test a theory, to assess its capacity to make correct predictions. If a theoretical prediction cannot be tied to a set of events or entities with what are termed *operational definitions,* the theory is virtually untestable. Its value in predicting can never be known. The hypothesis that God saves the souls of sinners when he feels generous is of no utility to science. We cannot point to events or phenomena around us that could either confirm or disconfirm such a hypothesis.

We shall not have to worry extensively about this problem of linkage in the present volume. However, there is a more subtle issue at stake that will become increasingly problematic as the book progresses. This is the issue of "psychologizing." A very important distinction can be made between theoretical terms that refer to processes, events, or structures *inside* the person, and terms that refer to overt behavior. Such terms as "feeling," "perception," "emotion," "cognition," and "thought" are of the former kind, while such terms as "body movement," "response increment," "attraction ratings," and "self-description" are of the latter. You may recall from earlier courses in psychology the notion of "hypothetical construct," a notion that has often been used to refer to processes or structures within the person to which we can have no direct access. If we accept the admonition that a theory is better insofar as its concepts refer to immediately observable events, then we must also conclude that hypothetical constructs are inferior as theoretical terms. This may be a bitter pill to swallow inasmuch as most of the terms we use in talking about why people do certain things, and most of the characteristics we feel to be crucial to us personally (our values, loves, aspirations), are considered hypothetical constructs. This is not to say that such terms must never be used. But the conditions under which they may be used should be limited, and the purist might wish to rule them out altogether.

Two conditions favorable for the use of hypothetical constructs may be elucidated by returning to our original research example. One theoretical speculation was that when the student was engaged in defending a position, he would think of supporting arguments for the position and against the opposition, and this process would cause him to become more committed to the position he was defending. The terms "think of supporting arguments" and "beliefs" fall into the category of hypothetical constructs. In what senses are they defensible?

First, there are observable operations that are designed to assess these ineffables. That is, we assume that certain types of overt behavior are indicative or are measures of these so-called internal events. Beliefs or "values" can be measured with questionnaires, as we have seen above; similarly, we could have subjects talk about or write down their "thoughts" in support of these beliefs. The hypothetical terms thus have a *second-order* anchor in reality. Second, such terms are helpful in explaining the results. They are *useful* and point to additional areas of relevant investigation. However, it must still be concluded that if an especially useful theory could be developed that did not rely on such constructs, it would be a better candidate for our attention.

3. *Extent of data base.* There is a small but active group of psychologists who feel that it is possible for people to send and receive information without making use of any of the normal senses, that is, by extrasensory means. However, the assumption is not shared by the majority of scientists in this country. They consider the theoretical assumption inferior, and seldom hesitate to criticize. Why should there be such a vehement reaction on the part of so many? What is it they find so objectionable?

The primary reason why people are loath to accept such a premise is that it violates the overwhelming evidence that science, as well as their daily lives, supplies to them. The term *antecedent probability* is often used in this context. In elementary form, it can be said that any theoretical prediction or hypothesis has a certain probability of being verified whenever it is tested. If a theory has had a history marked by successful predictions, the probability of its being correct in any new instance is quite high. In this case, it is said that the theory has a high antecedent probability. The degree to which there is a supportive data base contributes to the probability of its holding true in the present instance. Given the history of science to date, the ESP assumption has a very low antecedent probability. This is not to say that the theory is false, but simply that a considerable volume of data is required to establish a reasonable degree of antecedent probability. Resistance exists because accepting the ESP assumption means abandoning or drastically revising other theories of very high antecedent probability.

To return to the study of student values, how extensive was the data base underlying Brickman's theory? As it turns out, there is abundant evidence supporting the notion that publicly defending a position increases one's belief in that position. The literature dealing with the effects of role playing on attitude change is rife with examples. However, the study also assumed that the "folks" back home generally treat college students as examples of the college environment and cause them to defend the liberality found in the college setting. Here there is little supporting evidence, and this link in the reasoning remains untested. Perhaps you can examine your own experience and derive some intuitive feeling for the antecedent probability of the assumption.

4. Heuristic value. A theory may make accurate predictions, be linked to real-world events, and be based on abundant evidence, but at the same time essentially lead nowhere. The value of a theory in stimulating the field may be independent of these other considerations. The theorizing of Sigmund Freud is a good case in point. Psychoanalytic theory can hardly be said to have great predictive value (although it often proves handy after the fact); the concepts are difficult to pin down operationally; and the great controversy which it has created is a good indication of its low antecedent probability. And yet, almost all would agree that Freud's theory was one of the most significant contributions to Western thinking in the twentieth century. Why? Primarily because it has stimulated large numbers of investigators, both within the field of psychology and without, to develop new insights, generate discoveries, and restructure their research in more profitable ways. In effect, psychoanalytic theory is most important because of its heuristic value.

But what about the theorizing going into the study of student values? What heuristic value does it have? A moment's thought will reveal that the reasoning does lead in some interesting directions. For example, one might wish to investigate changes taking place in students' values as a result of going abroad. It is typically assumed that the *grand tour* broadens one's understanding, causes one to be more flexible, highlights the shortcomings in one's own narrow systems of belief. Does this always take place? Brickman's study suggests that there are circumstances under which a person returns home more committed to his narrowness than ever before.

5. Parsimony. It may be a commentary on human nature itself (although after reading enough psychology you may thoroughly disagree), but scientists generally hold that the briefer a theoretical statement the better. If two theories are equal in every other respect, the theory using the fewer theoretical terms is considered superior. Applying such a criterion might appear simple enough, but as you will see, application in practice is fraught with difficulty. In the first place, reality may be sufficiently complex that parsimony in any satisfactory sense is an impossible goal. The world may just not be amenable to understanding through simple propositions. In fact, the demand for parsimony can sometimes blind the investigator to subtle nuances within his data. Theories have a way of directing and guiding our perception. They cause us to be selective. And then again, even if an investigator realized that there were subtle findings that his theory could not account for, would it be worthwhile to add an entirely new set of concepts if 95% of his evidence supported his theory?

On another level, most hypothetical constructs are considered superfluous baggage by many theorists. They consider concepts such as love, hate, and anxiety unnecessary for understanding behavior, and advocate their banishment from the field of psychology. Having separate concepts to deal with the subjective experience of love as well as the overt expression of love seems a needless multiplication of terms. If you agree with the criterion of parsimony, you are at loggerheads with theorists who use such concepts. It should be noted in this respect that the theory applied to the data on student values is not very parsimonious. Many assumptions have to be made, many terms employed. Perhaps the rationale which you developed accounted for the data more succinctly.

These five criteria, then, are most important in evaluating a theory. There are other more ambiguous or less important criteria. For example, one might want to add the criterion of richness of the deductions made from a theory. A given theory might be extremely good in predicting behavior in an artificial laboratory setting. Many psychologists confine themselves entirely to such endeavors. When all theoretical deductions are relevant to the same situation, they may well become progressively more trivial. It is a matter of personal bias, but for many, a theory that has ramifications for a broad number of issues, both in and out of the laboratory, would be considered superior to one of limited scope. On much the same biased grounds, one could argue that a theory is more valuable if it has relevance to pressing social problems. However, what one calls "rich" in the way of theory depends primarily on his particular values and world outlook. One man's triviality may be another's god.

While on the topic of debate, you have no doubt realized that various theories may be good for different reasons. This raises the question of which criteria are more important. If a theory were based on solid factual evidence, but heuristically impoverished, for example, would it be better than an unsupported theory that stimulated many others in the field? There are no simple ground rules to follow in such situations. Suffice it for now that as we proceed we shall have to compromise a number of times among competing criteria. We shall simply have to negotiate such settlements, each within its own context. Armed with these criteria of evaluation, we are now prepared for the onrushing legions of abstraction.

REFERENCES

Brickman, P., Attitudes out of context: Harvard students go home. Undergraduate Honors Thesis, Harvard University, 1964.

Brown, R., *Explanation in Social Science*. Chicago: Aldine, 1963.

Direnzo, G. J. (ed.), *Concepts, Theory and Explanation in the Behavioral Sciences*. New York: Random House, 1966.

Janis, I. L., and B. T. King, The influence of role playing on opinion change. *Journal of Abnormal and Social Psychology,* **49**, 211-218, 1954.

Mandler, G., and W. Kessen, *The Language of Psychology*. New York: John Wiley and Sons, 1959.

Sarbin, T. R., Role theory, in *The Handbook of Social Psychology* (2nd edition, G. Lindzey and E. Aronson, eds.), Vol. I. Reading, Mass.: Addison-Wesley, 1968.

CHAPTER TWO

A Motivational Basis
for Social Behavior

In examining earlier thinking about the issues, you may have been struck by the premonition that our path would ultimately wend toward the early Greeks. The moment is at hand; but at least we shall not be obliged to conclude with the proverbial "nothing new has been added." Several hundred years before Christ, both Epicurus and Aristippus (a pupil of Socrates) developed a theory of human motivation that has continued to provide a challenge even to the present day. Boldly stated, the core assumption of the theory is that man is motivated by a single principle: to achieve pleasure and to avoid pain. In spite of many valiant attempts to find in man more lofty ambitions, thinkers over the centuries have never ceased to be haunted by the element of truth residing in this statement. As we shall see, the data of human behavior will require a vastly more complex form of this proposition, but the assumption nevertheless remains a cornerstone.

The foremost proponent of this position in Western philosophy was Jeremy Bentham, whose death in 1832 preceded Freud's birth by only 30 years. While a young man, Bentham wrote that human behavior is "under the governance of two sovereign masters, pain and pleasure." This statement came to play a major conceptual role in the well-known doctrine of hedonism, and in its ethical transformation, utilitarianism. It should be noted that Bentham's contemporary, Adam Smith, a classic economic theorist, proposed much the same motivational basis for economic behavior. As we shall see in a later chapter, Smith's early influence on economic theorizing forms the seedbed for important interpenetrations between contemporary psychology and economics.

Within early psychology the doctrine of hedonism was best represented in the work of Sigmund Freud and Edward Thorndike. For Freud, the search for pleasure and avoidance of pain was embodied in the concept of *primary process,* the basic principle guiding the flow of energy from the Id. For Freud, man's conduct was a by-product of the clash between the Id's attempt to maximize pleasure, and the multiple hurdles placed in the path of such goals by the social environment. For the early experimentalist, Edward Thorndike, the process of learning was primarily based on hedonic outcomes for the organism. That is, an animal learned new behavior principally when it allowed him to achieve pleasure or to avoid pain. Thorndike's statement that "pleasure stamps in; pain stamps out" has come to be widely known as the Law of Effect.

FROM HEDONISM TO SKINNERIAN BEHAVIORISM

In modified form, hedonism is most effectively represented today in the literature on the operant conditioning of animals, and in the theoretical formulations of B. F. Skinner. On the laboratory level, this work is clear and incisive and the results are dramatic. To take but one example: a pigeon is placed in a metal chamber. He struts about exploring his environment and at a random moment stretches his neck a little higher than usual. Suddenly, a grain of food appears in a tray below. Having gone without food for a number of hours, he quickly consumes the grain. He moves about, and after a brief interval, again raises his head; the grain appears and is quickly eaten. Within minutes a pattern of behavior begins to emerge. The animal begins soon after eating the grain to crane his neck, and this behavior takes place more and more rapidly and reliably. The experimenter may then withhold the grain and the bird will immediately seek new heights. And as the process proceeds, the pigeon attempts with great vigor to keep his head in the new position—careful to note the advent of grain, which is the only interruption to his maintaining the erect and awkward posture.

Thus, within a brief time, the experimenter has gained complete control over the bird's behavior. The bird's relaxed meandering has been replaced by a frenetic attempt to keep its head erect. If the experimenter were to withhold the grain for a long period, the behavior would disappear. In a sense, the pigeon is at the mercy of the environment, which may supply or withhold rewards at will. One needn't have a powerful imagination to see the implications of such techniques for the prediction and control of human behavior.

On a theoretical level, Skinner (1953, 1959) has matched such impressive techniques with an equally challenging theoretical departure. In the attempt to generate as parsimonious a theory as possible, and one that is closely linked with observable events, Skinner maintains that hypothetical constructs are unnecessary to predicting the behavior of organisms. In order to predict behavior, one need only assess the reinforcing properties of the stimulus world. Behavior is principally guided and controlled by reinforcing events in the environment. In the above example, the pigeon's behavior becomes dependent on the availability of grain. By controlling the time at which the reinforcement is presented, the amount of grain provided the animal, the consistency with which it is presented, and so on, the pigeon's behavior is controlled. What need then for such nonobservables as "drive," "hunger," "cognition," and "perception"? As Skinner has pointed out, "When we have achieved a practical control over the organism, theories of behavior lose their point . . . . When behavior shows order and consistency, we are much less likely to be concerned with physiological or mentalistic causes. A datum emerges which takes the place of theoretical phantasy." (1959, p. 375).

But what has happened to the classical principle of hedonism in this work? As you may have noticed, it has undergone an interesting transformation. Rather than concentrating on pleasure and pain, hypothetical constructs of the first rank, we find ourselves focusing on reinforcement properties in the environment. Skinnerian behaviorism is hedonism turned inside out. In addition to the gain in parsimony and reliance on real-world fact, this transformation is supported by a profoundly effective methodology. Should we then embrace these various elements of the behaviorist orientation? To what extent should they serve as essential ingredients in our theoretical recipe? Perhaps we should take a closer look.

The first difficulty emerges when one attempts to define reinforcement. Given that a major aim of science is to predict, or to formulate hypotheses that can be either verified or proven incorrect, one must use concepts that can be applied in advance of the actual occurrences one is interested in predicting. For example, in predicting the probability of rain, one typically uses the concept of "pressure." When high- and low-pressure areas collide, a high probability of rain is said to exist. The hypothesis of rain is testable if and only if one can provide identifying characteristics of high- and low-pressure areas that can be applied in advance of the rain itself.

The concept of reinforcement from the Skinnerian position does not lend itself to such advance specification. A reinforcement is defined as that which reinforces or causes a change in the probability of a behavioral occurrence. However, without evidence of the change in behavior, there is no way of identifying a reinforcement. In effect, the concept as it stands does not allow hypotheses to be tested. This is not to say that predictions can never be made. With good reason, psychologists in this area are confident that they can alter animal behavior in any of a number of pre-specified ways. The difference is, however, that such predictions are only statements that what has occurred in the past will recur if the conditions of the past are replicated. Without great familiarity with pigeons, for example, there would be no way of hypothesizing in advance that grain would reinforce pigeon behavior. A good theory of astrophysics, on the other hand, would predict rain as a result of pressure difference without ever having previous verification.

A second major problem has to do with the peculiar nature of "explanation" in the Skinnerian tradition. In the case of our stretch-necked pigeon, for example, the explanation for the bird's behavior might lie in the pattern and timing of reinforcement. That is, the experimenter might say that the pigeon's behavior was explained once the relationship between the neck stretching and reinforcement had been charted. Explanation, then, consists of isolating systematic relationships between environment and behavior.

However, this is a very peculiar sort of explanation. It is analogous to saying that when one has located certain mushrooms that cause death when eaten, he has explained deaths that occur from ingesting certain mushrooms. The functional relationship between the eaten mushroom and death, then, serves as the total explanation. The question of "why" is irrelevant. In the normal scientific tradition, the behavioristic type of explanation is viewed as a description rather than an explanation, and the question "why" is taken very seriously. In the case of the pigeon, one might develop a theory of hunger, concept learning, or physiology; with the mushroom, one might be interested in analyzing the chemical composition of the plant and its impact on the biochemistry of the body.

This latter approach not only satisfies our curiosity, but also has the advantage of maximum heuristic value. It leads to new investigations and suggests interesting links to other areas of concern. An adequate theory of hunger might lead us into speculating about the conditions under which grain would be maximally reinforcing to the pigeon, or about the differential impact of varying foodstuffs. If we understand the body's reaction to certain chemical compounds in the mushroom, we might also shed light on the effects of various other types of plants.

But should we abandon the behaviorist position altogether in favor of old-style hedonism? This alternative also seems unwise. The premise that all behavior is motivated by a desire for pleasure and an avoidance of pain is equally problematic. One major difficulty is that the premise is too abstract to make differential predictions. Simply saying that a man will seek his pleasure at a social gathering doesn't aid us in predicting whether he will gorge himself with food, guzzle the punch, or bite his hostess on the ear. Nor does the basic premise allow us to predict behavior in advance. The premise allows us only to speculate *after the fact* about what provided the most pleasure at least expense to the individual in a given situation. As we have said, there is a high premium on theories that predict.

Is there a viable alternative to classical hedonism, on the one hand, and Skinnerian behaviorism, on the other—an alternative that avoids the pitfalls but retains the positive features? Not altogether. But there is one that meets most of our earlier criteria for theory building, and which does provide us with invaluable leverage. The alternative is to break the seal, go into the organism, and develop a more differentiated theory of pleasure and pain. Instead of the gross concepts of pleasure and pain, we must begin to specify various types of pleasures or aversions. If we do not restrict ourselves to a literal translation of "pleasure and pain," the result can take the form of a set of needs or drives, each having slightly different physiological under-pinnings, and each being satisfied by specific types of reinforcement. In-vestigations stemming from such a theory would ultimately indicate the relative strengths of these drives in relationship to each other over time.

This solution is not parsimonious. Worse still, it requires the develop-ment of a large set of hypothetical constructs. However, it does retain the strength of the classic form of hedonism. Further, it would ultimately allow one to define reinforcement on *a priori* grounds, and to hypothesize in advance about the effects of varying types of reinforcements. Finally, it would provide an explanation in the more typical sense of the word. It would begin to tell us, for example, why grain affects pigeon behavior, and to point to conditions under which it might not. Finally, this alternative has considerable heuristic value, as the remainder of this volume should attest.

THE DRIVE-REDUCTION MODEL

The drive-reduction model in psychology is hardly a newcomer to the science. Its proponents have included some of the most eminent theorists in psychology (such as Clark Hull and Kenneth Spence). In elementary form, this approach first assumes that the behavior of the organism is in-fluenced by the operation of internal drives or tension-like states that seek reduction or relief. For many, this orientation has provided a clear mandate to isolate the various drives and to explore their workings.

Unfortunately for the social psychologist, the major focus of investiga-tion in this area has been on lower animals. Such study began in the early 1920's with a concentration on the relative strengths of various drives. For example, in a classic study carried out by Warden in 1931, observations were made of the number of times a laboratory rat would cross an electri-cally charged grid to receive certain rewards. This work showed that when thirst was at a maximum, the animal would cross the grid a greater number of times in a controlled period to receive water than it would to receive food when maximally hungry. The sex drive, however, proved less potent than either of the drives for hunger or thirst (though Freudians might wish to fault the relevance of the study because of the nature of the subject population). Interestingly enough, the strongest of the drives was the drive of the mother to be with her young—a drive without an immediately apparent physiological basis. Of additional note was the fact that the animal would cross the grid simply to explore the environment on the other side of the grid. This result forecast an entire line of research on what has been termed exploratory drive, or the organism's need for stimulation (cf. Berlyne, 1960).

More recent work has set aside the questions of "how many drives" and "how strong" to deal with the internal mechanisms at stake and the effects of various stimulus conditions on drive states. Investigations of the physiology of hunger, thirst, sleep, and stimulus deprivation in the human are all good examples of more recent attempts.

There are a number of sticky and as yet unanswered questions dealing with whether drive *reduction*, as opposed to consummatory activity or stimulation, is what the organism really seeks. However, more recent work by Collier and Myers (1961) and Miller (1963) promises that such problems may be solved. The question more vital to our concerns is how we may apply the drive-reduction model to social interaction. It is obvious that much social behavior is not immediately triggered by physiological or instinctual needs. An understanding of electrified grids and physiology doesn't immediately lend itself to an explanation of the rewards that many people find in dominance, competence, or social approval behavior. What additional ingredients are required?

THE LEARNED BASIS OF SOCIAL MOTIVATION

Again, the problem is one to which attention has been given in earlier times. The major distinction upon which we may draw is between native and learned needs or motives. While hunger, thirst, and sex fall into the former category, motivation for dominance, competence, approval, and the like would fall in the latter. The basic assumption in this case, and one supported by much evidence, is that learned motives are ultimately dependent on native motives for their establishment. New motives may be learned primarily because there are native reinforcers that the organism seeks.

What is the nature of this relationship between the two types of motivation? As an answer to this question you may already have in mind the two familiar models of conditioning: classical and instrumental. In the classical or Pavlovian conditioning paradigm, certain stimuli (unconditioned) elicit certain types of response (unconditioned) on a natural or unlearned basis. For example, meat powder presented to a dog evokes salivation. As you are well aware, any stimulus that appears in close association with an unconditioned stimulus will, over time, come to elicit some fraction of the unconditioned response. A bell (conditioned stimulus) sounded immediately prior to the presentation of the meat powder will itself come to elicit salivation. A behavioral reaction has been elicited, then, to a stimulus that was previously neutral. The dog has learned to salivate with the onset of the bell. Higher-order conditioning may also be achieved. For example, if a light is paired with the bell, salivation may ultimately be evoked by the appearance of the light alone.

The relevance of classical conditioning to the drive-reduction model quickly becomes apparent when it is realized that certain unconditional stimuli are capable of reducing biological needs or, on the other hand, of producing aversive reactions. Thus, any stimulus associated with such events may itself come to elicit some fraction of the "pleasure" or "pain" initially experienced by the organism. Watson and Raynor (1920) initially demonstrated this fact with an unfortunate child named Albert. Albert was inherently fearful of sudden, loud noises. When a white mouse to which the child was initially attracted was subsequently presented at the same time that a loud gong was sounded, the mouse alone eventually caused Albert to cry and to attempt an escape. Along more systematic lines, Miller (1948) later demonstrated that rats shocked in a white cage would subsequently go to great effort to escape this particular cage. One can think of dozens of parallels on the level of human social interaction: attraction to a person who has always been present when one has experienced pleasure, avoidance of groups in which one has experienced pain, and so on.

In turning to instrumental or operant conditioning as a source of learned motives, there is little to add to the belabored example of the pigeon discussed earlier. In this model the organism *learns* to behave in ways that will yield maximal reward in reducing biological drives or avoiding punishment. In order to understand the development of learned drives from this orientation, it is also necessary to realize that the organism may continue to behave in instrumental ways long after the behavior has ceased to be functional. The clearest case in animal work takes place when reinforcement is provided on an intermittent schedule and then removed altogether. For example, a pigeon might be taught to make a 360-degree turn in order to receive grain. If the grain is provided on an intermittent basis, such that not all 360-degree turns are rewarded, the pigeon may persist in his dizzy spinning for exceedingly long periods without reinforcement.

The implications for human behavior emerge more saliently when one considers Wolfe's (1936) early studies with chimpanzees. The chimps were taught that poker chips could be cashed in or used instrumentally to receive food. The question was whether, after this training, the animals would come to consider the chips valuable in themselves. The results indicated that the chimps would lift heavy weights in order to receive the tokens, even though food was not immediately available. More outstanding from the social standpoint, the animals would become rivals for chips. The larger animals would snatch them from the smaller; the males would often take all the chips belonging to the females. Without searching for morals, speculation about human behavior is indeed tempting. After all, don't we all have our own brand of chips—objects we seek or behaviors we engage in, for which the biological rewards are only vestiges of the past?

By this point you may be feeling a peculiar uneasiness in the fact that social psychologists must often support major underlying assumptions with animal studies. We often find principles of social interaction that do not hold up successfully from one subculture in society to another. How, then, can we begin to generalize from the pigeon, rat, and chimp to man? The following chapter is designed to reduce this uneasiness and, at the same time, to increase understanding of the potent control function played by social approval.

Before we get into the topic of social approval as a reinforcing agent, one cautionary note must be made. There are a number of terms often used to refer to those objects or events in the environment which reduce needs. Such objects or events are said to be *cathected* (invested with libidinal energy) in the Freudian brand of hedonism. Thorndike, however, used the terms "reward" and "punishment" to refer to the same environmental properties. The implication was that internal changes would take place when reward and punishment were experienced. These terms were later replaced by Skinner with the term "reinforcement." The latter term was useful because it pointed to the fact that objects or events in the environment could influence overt behavior. In the economic tradition of which Adam Smith was a progenitor, the term for reinforcement becomes "payoff" or "outcome." These terms do not carry with them the connotation that learning takes place, but they do imply that everything that provides pleasure or pain is the result of some action that a person takes. Both the terms "outcome" and "payoff" imply that the person has engaged in an activity which produces a result. In a sense, then, most of the terms normally used to talk about drive reduction are loaded—and in different ways. The connotations of each do point in useful directions, but to use any one of them alone tends to bias the case before we begin. For the sake of neutrality, we shall generally speak in terms of environmental events that produce "satisfaction" or "dissatisfaction." More specific terms can be used when the circumstances call for them.

REFERENCES

Allport, G. W., The historical background of modern social psychology, in *The Handbook of Social Psychology* (2nd edition, G. Lindzey and E. Aronson, eds.), Vol. I. Reading, Mass.: Addison-Wesley, 1968.

Bandura, A., and R. H. Walters, *Social Learning and Personality Development*. New York: Holt, Rinehart, and Winston, 1963.

Bentham, J., *An Introduction to the Principles of Morals and Legislation*. Oxford: Clarendon Press, 1879 (first published in 1789).

Berlyne, D. E., *Conflict, Arousal, and Curiosity*. New York: McGraw-Hill, 1960.

Cofer, C. N., and M. H. Appley, *Motivation: Theory and Research.* New York: John Wiley and Sons, 1965.

Collier, G., and L. Myers, The loci of reinforcement. *Journal of Experimental Psychology,* **61,** 57-66, 1961.

Freud, S., *The Basic Writings of Sigmund Freud* (A. A. Brill, ed. and transl.). New York: Random House, 1938.

Hull, C. L., *Principles of Behavior.* New York: Appleton-Century-Crofts, 1943.

Miller, N. E., Studies of fear as an acquirable drive: I. Fear as motivation and fear reduction as reinforcement in the learning of new responses. *Journal of Experimental Psychology,* 38, 89-101, 1948.

Miller, N. E., Some reflections on the law of effect produce a new alternative to drive reduction, in *Nebraska Symposium on Motivation.* Lincoln: University of Nebraska Press, 1963.

Miller, N. E., Liberalization of basic S-R concepts: extensions to conflict behavior, motivation and social learning, in *Psychology: A Study of a Science* (S. Koch, ed.), Vol. II. New York: McGraw-Hill, 1959.

Mowrer, O. H., *Learning Theory and Behavior.* New York: John Wiley and Sons, 1960.

Skinner, B. F., A case history in scientific method, in *Psychology: A Study of a Science* (S. Koch, ed.), Vol. II. New York: McGraw-Hill, 1959.

Skinner, B. F., *Science and Human Behavior.* New York: Macmillan, 1953.

Smith, A., *The Theory of Moral Sentiments.* London: A. Miller, 1759.

Spence, K. W., *Behavior Theory and Conditioning.* New Haven: Yale University Press, 1956.

Thorndike, E. L., *Animal Intelligence.* New York: Macmillan, 1911.

Watson, J. B., and R. Raynor, Conditioned emotional reactions. *Journal of Experimental Psychology,* 3, 1-14, 1920.

White, R. W., Motivation reconsidered: the concept of competence. *Psychological Review,* **66,** 297-333, 1959.

Wolfe, J. B., Effectiveness of token rewards for chimpanzees. *Comparative Psychological Monographs,* 12, No. 5, Whole No. 60, 1936.

CHAPTER THREE

The Impact of Social Approval

As we have seen, very little of the social interaction surrounding us seems motivated by biological necessity. However, in a great many instances we can put our finger on the learned drives that may be at stake. In fact, almost anyone asked about his major aims in life will respond with a set of goals that have been furnished to him by the culture and invested with value through learning experiences. Similarly, most of the values for which a person would give his life are of the same variety. One of the most powerful of these learned needs in contemporary society appears to be the need for social approval. The wide pervasiveness of this need is well illustrated by results from a recent survey of 1500 college students from some 37 colleges and universities.* The survey showed that only 9% of the students felt they often held their own view despite others' impatience, only 15% frequently ignored the opinions of their peers on matters of personal importance, and only 7% definitely did things without regard to the reactions of their peers. The noted personality theorist, Carl Rogers, has pointed out that not only is the need for positive approval or regard more powerful than biological needs for many individuals, but the inability to obtain acceptance is basic to many forms of mental illness.

Whether people need approval to a greater extent in this day and age than ever before, as suggested by David Riesman's *Lonely Crowd*, is a moot point. In terms of basic learning experiences, it seems that people learn to seek others' regard at an early age and have always done so. In the classical conditioning model, the warm acceptance of the mother may often accompany the satisfaction received in eating or tactile pleasure. In terms of

---

*Institutional Research Program for Higher Education, Educational Testing Service, Princeton, New Jersey.

instrumental conditioning, the child soon learns that the acceptance of his parents enables him to receive more basic rewards. After all, "please" and "thank you" are magic words, and the parents' pleasure upon hearing them is the key that unlocks many doors.

While the importance of social approval as a satisfier can hardly be denied, this chapter will allow us to explore the issue more thoroughly. First we shall look closely at studies showing how very subtle indicators of approval can modify behavior. We shall then discuss variations that are found in the need for approval. Approval does not have the same impact on all persons, nor the same impact on a single person over time. Exploring these issues will also bring us face to face with the rudiments of research methodology. Research methods are not inherently everyone's cup of tea, but without an appreciation of both the strengths and weaknesses of methods of fact finding, the full implications of a set of results cannot be grasped.

THE EFFECTS OF MINIMAL SOCIAL REINFORCEMENT

Social psychologists have not always appreciated the relevance of operant conditioning techniques when humans are involved. The behavior of rats and pigeons in an experimental chamber has often seemed remote from the complexities of human social life. And while it seemed fine that animal behavior could be shaped in mechanical fashion, it appeared that human beings after childhood would be little affected by such crude techniques. The awakening of relevance can perhaps be traced to 1955, and William Verplanck's work on the control of the content of conversation.

Verplanck's approach was simple but ingenious. Seventeen students in his class at Harvard sought out situations in which they were alone with one other person, and in which they could unobtrusively observe a clock and make doodles on a piece of paper. These conversations took place in dormitory rooms, restaurants, public lounges, and even over the telephone. During the first 10 minutes of any conversation the student-experimenter engaged his subject-friend in polite conversation, trying not to support or reject anything he had to say. At the same time, using a series of coded doodles, he carefully took note of the number of opinions which his unwitting friend expressed. After 10 minutes of this procedure, designed to establish the subject's base-rate of opinion responding, the experimenter went to work. It was his task to reinforce through social approval any statement of opinion which the subject made. As the conversation progressed, the experimenter would, after *any* opinion had been expressed, introject with comments such as "You're right," or "I agree," or he would simply nod his head and smile. At the same time, the experimenter would continue his doodling. After 10 minutes of this subtle flattery, extinction began. The experimenter would either fail to respond to opinion statements or disagree in the same subtle manner in which he had previously agreed.

If there is a highly pervasive need for social approval, and another's agreement is a satisfier for this need, the results of this study should be clear-cut. Statements of opinion should increase when they gain approval, and decrease when they elicit disapproval or neutrality. In fact, this is precisely what Verplanck found. All of the 24 subjects tested increased their rate of opinion expression when being reinforced, and 21 of the 24 showed a reduced rate in the extinction period. Such data were not only compelling, but Verplanck had managed to beat social psychologists at their own game. Social psychologists have long been worried by the fact that many of their principles are based on data obtained in the artificial confines of a laboratory, and here was an operant conditioning study that had successfully been conducted in a field setting.

Verplanck's study was not without its critics. After all, the experimenters were not professionally trained, nor was there any guarantee that they were professionally responsible. Had they done precisely what they were told to do, or what else might they have done to encourage or discourage opinion expression? And how accurate were their assessments of what constituted an "opinion"? Could these assessments have varied, depending on what they hoped they would hear? Verplanck also maintained the questionable position that subjects in his studies had been quite unaware of the fact that they were being manipulated.

These criticisms have led investigators in a number of directions. One major line of research, and one which has caused a good deal of controversy, has centered on the issue of awareness. Can a person's behavior be shaped without his being aware? This controversy is still being waged, with the majority of the evidence suggesting that the *greater* the subject's awareness of the contingencies of the situation, the more likely he is to respond with what he considers an appropriate answer.

Other investigators have attempted to improve on methodology. As you can well imagine, this aim has largely led to using artificial techniques in laboratory settings. Other researchers have attempted to reduce the amount of reinforcement to a bare minimum, primarily in order to ascertain whether learning can take place without awareness. Perhaps the most dramatic aspect of these studies is the way in which they demonstrate how much can be done to alter human behavior with only small amounts of social approval. It will prove enlightening to look more closely at one of the most interesting of these studies, conducted almost 10 years after Verplanck's initial work.

The setting of this investigation is again cut from real life. The employment interview is an experience that few can avoid during a lifetime, and large organizations frequently add a psychological interview to the hurdles that a job applicant must leap. In this case, a group of psychologists, whose primary interest was in shedding light on the little understood but vastly important processes of psychotherapy, were allowed to test Civil Service applicants under varying conditions. These investigators (Matarazzo, Saslow, Wiens, Weitman, and Allen, 1964) saw the clear parallels between the open-ended and nondirective job interview and the psychotherapeutic setting. The Civil Service also had an obvious interest in getting as much useful information from their applicants as possible.

The interviews were 45 minutes in length, allowing division into three equal periods (thus paralleling Verplanck's methodology). In the first 15-minute period, the clinical interviewer carried out the normal procedure, talking as little as he could while encouraging the applicant to talk about anything that came to mind. The second 15-minute period was conducted much as the first, with the single exception that each time the applicant began to say anything, the interviewer nodded his head slightly but affirmatively until the utterance had terminated. During this period, the interviewer might nod his head anywhere from 500 to 1000 times. In the third 15-minute interval the interviewer terminated the head nodding—perhaps out of exhaustion as well as for purposes of experimental rigor. Throughout the entire interview the psychologist took special care not to introduce other reinforcing stimuli, such as smiling or talking excessively with the interviewee.

The major interest of the study was the effect of the simple mechanism of head nodding on the duration of utterances. How long would the applicant continue to speak, as a result of the modest social approval communicated through the interviewer's head nodding? To insure that the obtained results were not limited by the fact that only one investigator could success-fully induce change, each of the senior investigators (Matarazzo and Saslow) interviewed 20 applicants, and their results were analyzed separately. The findings of the study are shown in Fig. 3.1. As you can see, head nodding had a strong effect on the duration of the applicants' speech. For the first interviewer, the effect of nodding his head during periods when the applicants were talking was to increase periods of talking by some 48%; for the second interviewer, the increase was 67%, and both increases were highly reliable on a statistical basis. In the third period, when the interviewer ceased nodding his head, the duration of talking also began to decrease, and again, the decrement proved statistically significant.

The experimenters had the additional wisdom to assess their own verbal output during the three periods. Why? Because one competing explanation of the results might be that their own verbal behavior could have influenced the applicants. If they talked for particularly long durations during the second period, as opposed to the first or third, for example, one could explain the results in terms of the applicants' modeling of the interviewer; if the interviewer talked for particularly brief intervals during the second period, one could say that his behavior simply left the applicants with more time to talk during this period. As the figure shows, neither explanation has any validity; both interviewers showed remarkably similar verbal patterns during all three time periods.

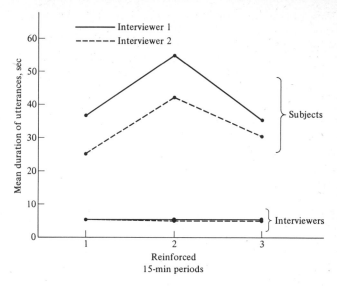

Fig. 3.1 The effects of affirmative head nodding on the duration of utterances in an interview. (Adapted from Matarazzo, Saslow, Wiens, Weitman, and Allen, 1964.)

Of course, there remains the question of why one interviewer generally produced a higher duration of speaking than his partner. And the first interviewer also used almost half the number of head nods, on the average, to produce the same increase as his partner. Clearly there are other aspects of the stimulus situation that one might wish to explore. Finally, you might wish to retain at least some doubt as to whether the major reinforcer was actually social approval. Head nodding could also be a signal to the applicant that what he was saying was important information and that he should continue to talk more about these topics. In an experiment we are soon to take up, our minds may partly be eased on this score.

WHEN IS SATISFACTION NOT SATISFACTORY?

If one were to examine at close range the data from the 40 subjects in the study by Matarazzo *et al.,* it would soon be apparent that not all the applicants responded in just the same way to the reinforcing properties of minimal approval. Some applicants were undoubtedly more responsive than others; long speech durations were extinguished more quickly for some than for others in the third 15-minute period. Although a number of extraneous variables might have been at play to create these differences among individuals, there is a more general issue at stake here. In order for our theoretical model to be in line with existing fact, it must be realized that a given satisfier does not have an equal effect on all persons at all times. If, furnished with the knowledge of the two studies just discussed, one were to begin applying subtle approval to his acquaintances in order to shape their behavior, he would often meet with disappointment. The predictive powers of the theory (and possibly one's social efficacy) could be greatly improved, however, by adding two major concepts: deprivation and satiation.

Deprivation and Satiation

The concepts of deprivation and satiation have a long history in psychology, particularly in the domain of animal experimentation. The need for these concepts becomes apparent very rapidly when one is dealing with physiological drives. An unfed or food-deprived animal will be far more reactive to food as a reinforcement than will an animal that has just eaten, or is satiated. In the same way, water will be more satisfying for an animal deprived of water, and a sexually responsive female rat more reinforcing for a sexually deprived male. The question is, however, whether those drives most important to understanding social behavior, the learned drives, operate in the same fashion. In the case of the need for social approval, will a person who has been deprived or satiated be more or less responsive to approval from others?

Insofar as we have data available, the answer to this question seems to be yes. You might first examine your own experience for supporting evidence. Perhaps there have been times when you have been extremely grateful for the kind or accepting word of another. It is quite possible that these times were preceded by your having been criticized, ostracized, or socially rejected. There may also have been times in which approval has been received with indifference. Possibly these have been times when your pride has just been inflated. In some cases, you may even have found that you dislike social approval. We might thus speak of extreme forms of satiation as *saturation*—a point after which an additional satisfier may be aversive.

To be more systematic, in dealing with learned needs two factors determine one's relative degree of deprivation or satiation. The first can be traced to the long-term history of the organism, and the second to the immediate situation in which he finds himself. In the first case, persons may differ with respect to how much of a given satisfier they have learned to require. Some persons may be predisposed, as a result of early experience, to require a good deal more of a given satisfier than others. Such persons exist in what may be viewed as a *chronic* or continuous state of deprivation. In the second case, the environment in any given period may provide or withhold satisfaction. The amount of satisfaction received in that brief period should have a significant effect on the person's needs at the moment. Needs in this sense may be viewed as *situationally dependent*. Receiving a high rate of social approval in a short span of time should lead to satiation, and the satisfier should thus become less and less reinforcing. However, we should not continue to deal in "shoulds." Rather, we may examine two studies, each of which sheds light on one of these cases.

The Chronic State: Need Approval

continued in ... *presented*

The state of chronic need for social support has been discussed for a good many years in psychiatric circles. Karen Horney, Erich Fromm, and more recently Carl Rogers have discussed at length the person with a deficit in social acceptance or approval. It has been felt that a long-term deficit causes depression, anxiety, and defective interpersonal relations. The desirable state, from the psychiatric point of view, is one in which the person has a sufficient level of self-regard that he does not require the continued approval of others. While there seems to be much wisdom in these arguments, it is another matter to set about studying chronic deficits in approval in a systematic, empirical manner. Clinical evidence alone is hardly sufficient. There is no hypothesis, however improbable, for which support cannot be found in the clinic.

But how can one begin such an exploration? The manipulation of childhood environments to produce long-term deficit or satiation is not only impracticable, but unethical. Longitudinal studies of child-rearing habits are feasible. However, at the initial stages of research they are problematic; there is little clue at this point as to precisely what one should be observing.

One of the most promising strategies is to isolate certain types of adult behavior that display characteristics indicative of the approval need. Once such behavior has been identified, its stability across time and circumstances can be assessed with an eye toward evaluating whether or not it can be viewed as chronic. Differences in the amount of this behavior from person to person can then be related to other behaviors considered indicative of approval motivation. If high correlations are generally obtained, one can feel more secure in the assumption that the initial behavior chosen for study is indeed an indicator of approval needs; i.e., greater antecedent probability would have been established. At this point, cases with extreme scores on the measure might be selected and data collected on their past history. It would be safest in this case to cast a broad net for any past experiences that would reliably differentiate the extreme high scorers from those lowest in need approval. Results derived from this type of investigation can then be used for more intensive examination of child-rearing habits and peer-group relations over time. Ultimately, the result should be a much increased understanding of the causes and effects of approval needs.

This is not to say, however, that someone has actually carried through this series of steps. However, there are two investigators, David Marlowe and Douglas Crowne, who have gone a good part of the distance. This is not the place for a complete examination of their work (cf. Crowne and Marlowe,

1964), but a brief account of their confrontation with issues of measurement and prediction will nicely illustrate the major points being made in this section.

Their research program was originally triggered by one of the major insights of the past 10 years in the field of psychological testing. As you are all too painfully aware, one stock-in-trade for many psychologists is the paper-and-pencil test in which the respondent is asked a variety of questions about himself. For many years it has generally been assumed that people respond to the content of such questions. If asked about whether they drive a car, for example, it is assumed that they will consider the content of the question before responding "yes" or "no." The major breakthrough came when it was found that people were highly prone to answer questions on stylistic grounds that operated over and above the effects of content. Such stylistic approaches have been called *response sets,* and have included the tendency to answer questions in the affirmative, or to answer questions with extreme answers, regardless of the specific meaning of the questions.

Marlowe and Crowne concentrated on differences among people in their tendency to answer questions in a socially desirable way. Almost any question you can think of has one answer that is more generally desirable or socially acceptable than another. The question that these investigators raised, however, was what function socially desirable responding plays in the person's life. What does it indicate about the person when he answers questions, regardless of content, in a socially acceptable way? Essentially, they reasoned that a person who answers in such a way as to elicit praise or approval from others is one who has a chronic need for social approval.

To explore this possibility Marlowe and Crowne developed a "true-or-false" test composed of 33 items, each of which had one answer earmarked as more socially desirable than the other. For example, if a person answered "true" to the question, "I am always careful about my manner of dress," and "false" to "I like to gossip at times," he would have answered in the socially desirable way. As you can see, the motivation to answer in this manner would have to be very high indeed. The socially desirable response typically ensnares the person in a "little white lie" about himself. After all, is there anyone who is *always* careful about his manner of dress, or *never* indulges in gossip?

The investigators then asked whether people's scores on the test were reliable over time. In general, high correlations were found to exist between scores on the test from one month to the next. The next question was whether test scores, supposedly indicative of the degree of chronic need for approval, would relate to other behavior generally thought to be indicative of approval motivation. One of the most compelling of these studies was carried out by Crowne and Strickland (1961), an investigation that is historically related to the Verplanck study and that provides excellent support for the concept of chronic need states.

Subjects in this experiment, introductory psychology students at Ohio State, were instructed by the experimenter simply to say words—all the words that came to mind—without using sentences or phrases and without counting. This task undoubtedly seemed innocuous enough to subjects (except to those who were familiar with the free-association method in psychoanalysis). The subjects were exposed at random to one of three different treatments. In the first, termed the *Positive Reinforcement* condition, the experimenter reacted with a subtle "mm-hmm" and an affirmative but slight nod of the head each time the subject uttered a plural noun. This minimum approval reaction to plural nouns was maintained for a full 25 minutes. The second group of subjects were exposed to negative reinforcement. Rather than an affirmative response, the experimenter replied to all plural nouns with a negatively toned "uh-uh." The third group served as controls, and they simply went on saying words for the full 25 minutes.

The major interest of the study was the reaction of persons deemed high or low in need approval to differences in social reinforcement. Subjects were thus divided into two groups, depending on whether they were above or below the median of the distribution of test scores, and the proportion of plural nouns they emitted during each 5-minute period of the experiment was tallied. The effects of positive reinforcement or approval can be found in Fig. 3.2. It is immediately noticeable that need approval, as measured by the Marlowe-Crowne scale, predicts reactions to positive reinforcement quite accurately. High-need-approval subjects show an increment in proportion of plural nouns during the first 5 minutes, and this increment over low-need-approval subjects is maintained throughout the 25-minute session. The results are highly reliable on a statistical basis.

Also plotted in Fig. 3.2 are the results obtained in the control condition. In this condition, where no approval was given by the experimenter, no difference was found to exist between high- and low-need-approval subjects. In fact, if anything, in a normal interview the high-need-approval subjects seem to use proportionally fewer plural nouns. Those subjects who are chronically low in need approval respond the same way under reinforcement as they do without it.

Turning to the results in the *Negative Reinforcement* condition, we find a mirror image of the above. High-need-approval subjects are much more affected by minimal disapproval for plural nouns. They respond with fewer and fewer as the procedure progresses. Low-need-approval subjects, on the other hand, are almost indifferent to negative reinforcement. They behave in a manner quite similar to nonreinforced subjects. High need approval predisposes one, then, not only to engage in behavior that elicits minimal approval from others, but to avoid doing that which yields even the slightest disapproval.

These results also furnish good illustrations of the proposition with which this discussion began: there are important variations in the degree to

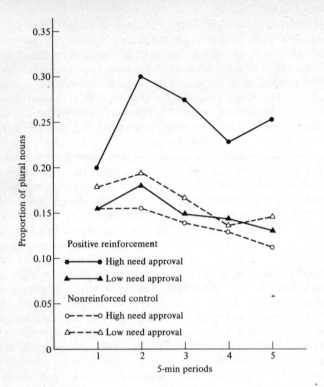

Fig. 3.2 Need approval and reactions to positive reinforcement. (From Crowne and Marlowe, 1964.)

which persons receive satisfaction from social approval. At the same time, the study lends validity to the measure in question, and further justifies our previous argument that very subtle forms of agreement from another serve as signifiers of social approval. As a final irony, it is extremely interesting to note that later work by Marlowe, Crowne, and their associates indicates that those persons who are most in need of social approval are least likely to acquire it. In a number of separate studies, those persons who have scored highest on the measure have been found to be least popular among their peers. Why this is true and what types of early experiences engender this condition of chronic need are questions that research has not yet answered.

The Situationally Dependent State

It has been pointed out that the satisfaction value of social approval may depend not only on the needs of the person developed over time, but also on what he has received in the immediate situation. The most obvious parallel in the case of biologically based needs is hunger. Food has great value to the person as a satisfier if he has gone for a prolonged period without it. After a large meal, food has little value for the person, and indeed, its presence may even be aversive. Consider a foot-long hotdog after your next Thanksgiving dinner. Why learned needs should follow the same pattern as biological needs, however, is not clear. One cannot easily use knowledge of biological needs and their operation to make deductions about learned needs. But we should hold this question in abeyance until we have had an opportunity to examine research findings.

One of the clearest expositions of the dependency of learned need states on the immediate situation stems from work on the social behavior of children. Focusing on children is additionally valuable in pointing up the early genesis of needs for social approval in the life of the person. In one particular study, Gewirtz and Baer (1958) selected a group of 102 middle-class children from the first and second grades. Both boys and girls participated in roughly equal numbers. Subjects were randomly assigned to one of three conditions: a *Deprivation* condition in which they were systematically deprived of social approval, a *Saturation* condition in which they received an abundance of approval, or a *Nondeprivation* condition in which they were neither deprived nor saturated.

How were these conditions arranged operationally? In the Deprivation condition, a female experimenter came to the classroom to bring the child to the experiment. As they walked the several hundred feet down the corridor to the experimental room, the experimenter said as little as possible. After they had reached their destination she told the child that the game he was to play was temporarily in use and that he would have to wait for a short time. The child was then left alone for a period of 20 minutes. In the Saturation condition, children were confronted with quite a different state of affairs. During the long walk the experimenter maintained a pleasant and interested attitude toward the child at all times; she praised and admired the child as much as possible. During the 20-minute wait the child was given pictures or cut-out designs with which to play. For the entire period the experimenter steadily administered praise and admiration at whatever the child did or said about himself. During the 20-minute period each child received approximately 30 such reactions. In the Nondeprivation condition, subjects were treated much as they were in the Deprivation condition during their walk to the experimental room, but they were not exposed to the 20 minutes of isolation. Instead, they were immediately allowed to play the game.

The game, presented to all the children, consisted of a large angular box into which the child dropped marbles. The marbles could be dropped into either one of two holes at the top of the box, and they returned to an open tray at its base. During the first four minutes of play, the experimenter remained silent except to answer any questions the child might have. During the fourth minute, however, the experimenter carefully observed which of

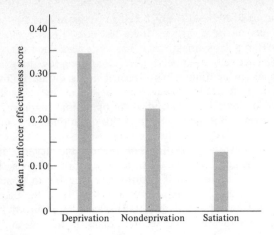

Fig. 3.3 Approval as a reinforcer and prior need state. (From Gewirtz and Baer, 1958. Copyright 1958 by the American Psychological Association, and reproduced by permission.)

the two holes the child tended to favor or to use most frequently. During the 10 minutes that followed, the experimenter then began systematically to administer approval on a fixed ratio schedule (in which a fixed proportion of responses were reinforced) whenever the child used the hole that had been least preferred during the fourth minute. This approval took the form of words such as "good," "hmm-hmm," or "fine."

The major interest of the study was the relative effects of the different levels of prior approval on the children's choice behavior. To gauge the impact of the approval, a "reinforcer effectiveness" score was derived for each subject. This score essentially reflected the increase, from the fourth minute of the game through the reinforced period, in the proportion of marbles dropped into the "correct" hole. Figure 3.3 displays the reinforcer effectiveness means for subjects in each of the three conditions. As the figure shows, the amount of social approval received prior to the marble game had a marked influence on children's responsiveness to reinforcement in the game itself. Those children who had been deprived of social approval beforehand were most affected by approval as a reinforcer during the game itself. Interestingly enough, subjects who had been satiated were even less responsive than the control or Nondeprivation subjects.

Additional light is shed on the scene by further results reported by Gewirtz and Baer. During the first four minutes of the game a count was also taken of the number of times the child attempted to initiate conversation with the experimenter. Specifically, the frequency with which the child commented, questioned, or otherwise sought attention was assessed with the view in mind that each of these various behaviors would be indicative of the extent to which the child needed social approval at that time. (The Saturation condition could not be considered in this analysis because in this condition only, the experimenter had already struck up a friendly interchange with the child. Here the initiation of conversation might be the result of their degree of acquaintanceship and not of need for approval.) When the number of attempts to initiate conversation in the Deprivation condition was compared with the number of attempts made in the Nondeprivation condition, children in the former condition were found to initiate significantly more interchange (a mean of 4.4 in the Deprivation condition, as compared to 2.3 in the Nondeprivation condition). Thus, children who were most influenced by social approval as a reinforcing agent also initiated a greater amount of interaction.

Although subject to criticism, these results lend good support to our general proposition that the value of a given satisfier may be altered within a situation. Now that we have examined some of the most compelling evidence, perhaps you are convinced that learned drives operate in much the same way as biologically based drives. However, if this is true, we are left with an enigma: why should they? In the case of biological drives, research has consistently revealed physiological or biochemical processes that account for altered states of drive level. In the case of hunger, thirst, and sleep, for example, subcortical areas have been found to play a crucial role in momentary need state. No such mechanisms are apparent in the case of learned drives.

While we are in no position to answer this question once and for all, speculation can be hazarded. It may be that the individual learns to identify what might be viewed as an *optimal state*. This optimal state may be socially defined and dependent on his learning the dominant values of the subculture in which he lives. For example, one subculture may value high rates of giving and receiving approval, while another may feel quite arbitrarily that lesser amounts are desirable. What the contemporary American feels is *sufficient* may differ from what the early colonists regarded as desirable. Thus, the value of a given satisfier can be seen as dependent on the cultural or subcultural norms. Receiving less satisfaction than the person feels is necessary would be defined by him as a state of deprivation, and would result in an increase in the person's activity and responsiveness to the satisfier. Amounts that greatly exceed the norm might thus be devalued also.

On the other hand, it is possible that the person becomes dependent on environmental constancy. That is, it is not a given class of satisfier that has value, but simply a moderately *constant* amount of whatever outcomes the person may be receiving. Recent research on both animals and human beings is beginning to indicate that an environment providing random outcomes or a high degree of unpredictability is emotionally detrimental to the organism. Inconsistency or, in its extreme form, unpredictability may even be a biologically aversive state. From this viewpoint, it might be hypothesized that the person with a high chronic need for approval is really seeking an amount of approval that is consistent with an earlier childhood state. In other words, those who most need the acceptance of others as adults may be those who have had *more* acceptance as children, not less, as is often thought.

Given the current lack of definitive explanation, we might usefully resort to a descriptive concept developed by Thibaut and Kelley (1959). They have coined the term *comparison level* (CL) to deal with the problem of the relative value of satisfiers. They point out that the person operates as if he compares the outcomes obtained at a given moment with a standard. Outcomes below the standard are dissatisfying and those above provide satisfaction. For these theorists, the CL is determined by what the person has experienced in the past and what he has seen others experience. This standard of judgment can be modified not only by past experience, either long-term or short-run, but also by cues in the present environment. In effect, the person may be reminded of certain outcomes he has experienced or that others are experiencing, and the salience of these cues may affect his current standards of judgment.

Although a valuable aid to understanding, the concept of CL alone does not take us far enough. For one thing, people appear to accept negative outcomes in a long-term relationship without reacting punitively or attempting to leave the relationship. In many marriages both husbands and wives complain bitterly and continuously, and yet the marriages never reach the divorce courts. There seems, then, to be a broad range of negative outcomes below CL that a person will tolerate without marked behavioral reaction. Thibaut and Kelley also recognize this fact and utilize the concept of *comparison level for alternatives* (CL_{alt}) to deal with it. The comparison level for alternatives is a separate standard of judgment which the person is said to use in evaluating his outcomes in one relationship in comparison with what he might expect to receive if he removed himself from this relationship. The person will maintain himself in a continuous state of dissatisfaction, it is said, so long as his comparison of the alternatives continues to convince him that he is in an optimal position. Poor marriages often continue because the alternatives (e.g., divorce proceedings, living alone, social criticism, and so on) present an even bleaker picture.

In addition, the concept of CL does not account for what we have termed a saturation point—that point beyond which outcomes normally considered positive become aversive. People may learn to value social approval, power, freedom of action, and so on; but for each of these there seems to be a point beyond which additional satisfaction from the environment is painful. In the long run, it may be more parsimonious to abandon the concept of CL_{alt} and to think in terms of the comparison level as a midpoint in a range of acceptable outcomes. Outcomes markedly above or below the midpoint may be aversive. Whether this range is particularly narrow on the negative side or extended on the positive, or whether it is easier to shift CL in the more positive than in the more negative direction, would be matters of empirical concern.

Thus far we have considered the genesis of social motives, and seen something of the way in which their gratification molds and directs behavior. We are now in a position to turn to the more complex problems that arise when we consider two persons—in relationship to each other—each struggling for gratification.

REFERENCES

Crowne, D. P., and D. Marlowe, *The Approval Motive.* New York: John Wiley and Sons, 1964.

Crowne, D. P., and B. R. Strickland, The conditioning of verbal behavior as a function of the need for social approval. *Journal of Abnormal and Social Psychology,* **63**, 395-401, 1961.

Gewirtz, J. L., and D. M. Baer, Deprivation and satiation of social reinforcers as drive conditions. *Journal of Abnormal and Social Psychology,* **57**, 165-172, 1958.

Horney, Karen, *Neurosis and Human Growth.* New York: Norton, 1950.

Krasner, L., and L. P. Ullmann, *Behavior Influence: The Effect of Social Reinforcement on Individual Behavior.* New York: Holt, Rinehart, and Winston, 1966.

Krasner, L., and L. P. Ullmann, *Research in Behavior Modification.* New York: Holt, Rinehart, and Winston, 1967.

Matarazzo, J. D., G. Saslow, A. N. Wiens, M. Weitman, and B. V. Allen, Interviewer head-nodding and interviewer speech deviations. *Psychotherapy,* **1**, 54-63, 1964.

Rogers, C. R., *On Becoming a Person.* Boston: Houghton Mifflin, 1961.

Thibaut, J. W., and H. H. Kelley, *The Social Psychology of Groups.* New York: John Wiley and Sons, 1959.

Verplanck, W. S., The control of the content of conversation: reinforcement of statements of opinion. *Journal of Abnormal and Social Psychology,* **51**, 668-676, 1955.

Wolpe, J., and A. A. Lazarus, *Behavior Therapy Techniques.* New York: Pergamon Press, 1967.

CHAPTER FOUR

Interdependence and Accommodation

The analysis thus far may not seem very *social* in nature. Essentially we have concentrated on the behavior of single individuals stimulated to behave in certain ways. Individuals have been reinforced, for example, for using plural nouns, talking for longer periods, or making decisions in a marble game. The experimenter has provided the cause for the behavior and observed the effects which he has created. However, as we look about us we seldom observe these sorts of occurrences. Instead, we see people *interact*. Their behavior is interdependent. One behaves toward another, who reacts to affect the initiator, and so on, for sequences that may go on continually for many years. Instead of concentrating solely on the reactions of individuals to a single stimulus provided by an experimenter, an approach that Sears (1951) has called *monadic,* we need to expand our efforts. Most especially, we must focus on *dyadic* relationships involving the mutual give and take of at least two persons over time.

The emphasis on the dyadic process also leads us headlong into one of the most distinctive properties of the social exchange approach to interpersonal behavior. Thus far we have treated only the needs of the single individual in a social setting. We have said that another's behavior may provide satisfaction to him, and in that respect be valuable to him. In the dyadic situation, we broaden our perspective to look at the needs of both members of the dyad. Here we observe that person A's behavior may have some value for B, but that B's reaction to A's behavior may satisfy or fail to satisfy A. In this sense, behavior is exchanged between A and B. If we look at a verbal conditioning experiment, such as we described in Chapter Three, we concentrate only on the reaction of B, the subject, to social approval provided by A, the experimenter. In so doing, we completely lose sight of possible effects of B's reactions on A, or effects that B might have been attempting to produce in A. In fact, the experimenter is sometimes loath to recognize properties of exchange in psychological experiments of this variety. He is threatened by the fact that the most important thing to him in such a situation is that his hypothesis is confirmed. He might thus subtly communicate this to the subject in such a way that the subject will behave "appropriately" in order to please him, and thus to receive the implied approval.

THE INTERACTION MATRIX AND THE RUDIMENTS OF EXCHANGE

The dyadic relationship can be represented visually in a very useful way. First we might consider the entire range of activities in which persons A and B are capable of engaging in the relationship. In Fig. 4.1, for example, A's repertoire of various behaviors is represented as $a_1, a_2, \ldots, a_n$; B's possible behaviors in the same situation are represented as $b_1, b_2, \ldots, b_n$. Now we can further assume that any behavior in which A engages will provide him with a certain degree of satisfaction or dissatisfaction. He may have a learned need to be aggressive and then derive satisfaction from tormenting his mate, or he may have learned to dislike serious conversation and thus find himself quite dissatisfied when meeting his friend at the local coffee-house. Similarly, B's various activities will provide him with various amounts of satisfaction or dissatisfaction.

We can further assume that it may ultimately be possible to quantify the satisfaction value of given types of behavior. We have already seen that

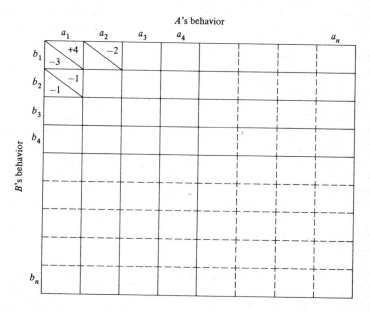

Fig. 4.1 The interaction matrix.

this is potentially possible in the case of the number of times a rat would cross an electrified grid in order to reduce various need states. While the methodology for reducing human needs to a simple scale is not immediately apparent (you might imagine trying to compare along a single dimension a lobster dinner, a peace demonstration, and the chance to avoid a midterm exam), the possibility seems reasonable in theory. If we assume that such a common hedonic scale can be developed, we can assign numerical values to each of the behaviors in which the person might engage. Satisfaction can be represented by positive integers, dissatisfaction by negative integers, with a neutral point at zero. Thus, the amount of satisfaction that A receives from tormenting B (behavior a_1 in the diagram) might provide A with satisfaction equaling +4, while serious conversation (a_2) might provide him with dissatisfaction equaling -2. These values or outcomes are represented in the various cells of the matrix formed by the array of various A and B behavior combinations. Similar entries could conceivably be made for the entire repertoire of both A's and B's activities.

Although this formulation may appear quite straightforward up to this point, one can always depend on the "reasonable" to be problematic. For one, as we have seen, the satisfaction value of a given behavior may vary across time and circumstances. The value of aggressiveness may be altered after one has aggressed (the essence of the cathartic experience), the value of being loved increased when one cannot find love. This means that the values entered into our diagram are not constant, but highly variable. The matrix over time is a constantly shifting field. A second problem arises in the fact that a given behavior may provide multiple satisfactions and dissatisfactions. Eating a lobster dinner for most people carries a high degree of satisfaction. But this satisfaction may not be limited to one's hunger drive; additional pleasure might be provided to the senses of smell, taste, and touch. In addition, a lobster dinner has a certain cultural value attributed to it ("snob appeal"), and one might gain additional gratification in this way. At the same time, the dinner has certain dissatisfactions associated with it. At the outset there is the cost in dollars, and therefore a reduction in other things the person is free to do. In a day in which social inequality is made so painfully apparent, such a meal might also engender the dissatisfaction of guilt.

Most theorists have dealt with this latter difficulty by assuming that satisfiers and dissatisfiers summate arithmetically. Thus, in order to ascertain the total amount of satisfaction, one would add the various satisfiers and subtract the dissatisfiers to arrive at a final total. The analogy of the market place has proved a useful one here. Satisfaction can be looked at as *benefit* and dissatisfiers as *costs*. The difference between the two can be looked at as *profit* or as *loss* (Homans, 1961), depending on which is the larger. A person may "profit" psychologically from eating the lobster dinner, because the amount of pleasure derived exceeds his concern with money or social inequality. Such an assumption also lends itself to looking at the parallels between profit motivation in business and behavior in other sectors of the social world. But now to the crucial question. Is it justifiable to add satisfiers and subtract dissatisfiers in a simple arithmetic fashion?

Even if the various satisfactions were quantifiable, it does not follow that they are necessarily additive, and that a given amount of satisfaction is simply canceled by an equal amount of dissatisfaction. In fact, the state in which roughly equal amounts of satisfaction and dissatisfaction derive from the same behavior is often termed "conflict." The term itself implies that such a state is aversive and undesirable. Thus, positive and negative outcomes stemming from the same behavior may interact, and the total result may be one of considerable dissatisfaction. In effect, the economic analogy is misleading in its simplicity, and ultimately a more fine-grained analysis will be necessary for viable predictions to be made.

Keeping these difficulties in mind, we can return to complete the basic description of our diagram. What has been said thus far is that for every behavior in which a person engages, there is some degree of satisfaction or dissatisfaction which he experiences, and that degree of satisfaction may ultimately yield to precise quantification. Two sources of satisfaction may be distinguished. On the one hand, there are hedonic outcomes that are *intrinsically* produced. They depend on what the person himself does and not on the behavior of the other person in the situation. As such, these outcomes may be contrasted with those which are *extrinsic*. Satisfaction or dissatisfaction of an extrinsic sort is that experienced as a result of the behavior of the other person. In the diagram, the pleasure that our dull but sadistic A is receiving from being hostile (the +4 in the a_1 category) is at the same time being experienced as pain or dissatisfaction by B (represented by the -3 in b_1). While A is receiving intrinsic rewards for his aggression, B is experiencing extrinsic punishment from passively "taking it."

It is at this point that the concept of exchange becomes central. Person B's "taking it" in the above case also has extrinsic value for A. Person A derives intrinsic pleasure not only from his own activity, but also from B's simultaneous passivity. If, on the other hand, B's behavior caused A to feel guilty, we might want to reduce the +4 that A is receiving for behavior a_1 to +1 in order to account for the extrinsic effect of B on A. Rather than alter the diagram to represent such a possibility, we might consider another reaction that B might have in his repertoire, namely hostility. Hostile behavior on his part (b_2) might give him a little more pleasure (or at least less dissatisfaction) than being passive (-1). At the same time, this activity may reduce further the pleasure that A is receiving for being aggressive. Thus, the +1 which he had been receiving might be reduced to a -1. In this case, both are receiving a certain amount of dissatisfaction from their mutual interaction. By taking into account the sources of pleasure and displeasure and exchange of behavior, we have considerably increased our understanding of the relationship.

With the development of the interaction matrix, our scope begins to expand rapidly. If we consider the entire behavioral repertoire of any two persons, and we know what behaviors are intrinsically rewarding to them, we can first begin to predict the type of behavior each will lean toward or prefer. If we can then assess the extrinsic rewards each might derive from the other's preferred behaviors, we would further be able to predict the amount of mutual satisfaction each might experience with the other. If one receives major satisfaction from dominating, and the other enjoys submissiveness, we might well expect a successful relationship.

If the satisfaction a person is experiencing in a given activity is related to the frequency with which he will engage in that activity, a fundamental axiom in the hedonic tradition (Homans, 1961), one could also predict the longevity of a relationship. If dominance is rewarding, the individual should attempt it more often, and thus continue also to provide rewards to his submissive mate. As you can see, our model has suddenly led us into heartland for the social psychologist. It begins to tell him what he might begin to look for in understanding the formation and longevity of friendship, cohesiveness in small groups, courtship and marriage, and race relations. The formulation begins to point to important aspects of leadership development, compatability in groups, work performance in teams, and even, possibly, relations among nations. But we must be cautious and not prematurely indulge ourselves in imperialistic fantasy. The basic foundations must be laid much more carefully and sealed with the cement of empirical findings before we can move any further.

The remainder of this chapter will attempt to move us in the direction of establishing such foundations. First, we shall discuss an investigation that lends factual support to a number of the basic concepts laid out thus far. This will lead us to expand our horizons ever so slightly to deal with interaction over time and the issue of sequence. The chapter following will allow us to move further into the research domain.

ACCOMMODATION IN A MINIMAL RELATIONSHIP

What are some of the initial questions raised by the matrix model developed above? You have seen how rapidly these elementary notions could be brought to bear on issues of widespread significance. But what checks would you wish to perform before proceeding to this grand level? And catering to standards of methodological rigor, how would you go about making these assessments?

One of the major assumptions stemming from the above is that over time two persons will tend to engage in behavior providing the greatest common satisfaction. In essence, they should accommodate themselves to each other in such a way as to provide *maximum joint payoff*. This follows if it is assumed that each of the persons would attempt first to maximize satisfaction and would then have to modulate this behavior in accordance with the other person's reaction. The conversation of a couple on their first date, for example, might range over a variety of topics, with each of the participants choosing first a topic from which he or she received most pleasure. If the reaction of the other were apathetic, a less pleasurable alternative might be sought until the couple eventually centered on interests that were mutually benefiting (or least dissatisfying to both).

To test the basic assumption of accommodation, it would also be advantageous to develop a methodology that penetrates the extraneous and unessential to get to the heart of the matter. Working with the entire behavioral repertoire of two persons and gauging the satisfactions for each behavior for each of the parties would not only be cumbersome, but at present the measurement problems would also be insurmountable. A most promising way to proceed might thus be to collapse the spectrum of behaviors available to the two persons and to arrange the situation in such a way that the satisfactions engendered by each behavioral alternative are specified by the experimental situation. This is precisely what Sidowski, Wyckoff, and Tabory (1956) did in what might be considered the single most conservative test of the accommodation assumption.

Subjects in this study (again unfortunate elementary psychology students) were led to an isolated chamber where electrodes were attached to the fingers of the left hand. In front of the subject were two buttons and a point-counter. The subject was told he could push either of the two buttons he wished and as frequently as he wished. He was also told that he might on occasion expect shock from the electrodes, or, on the other hand, points to accumulate on his counter. It was his task to make as many points as possible. The investigators took it for granted that he would be motivated to avoid shock to the same degree. The subject was then left alone in this mechanical void for 25 minutes.

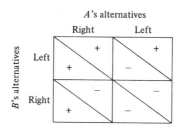

Figure 4.2

In actuality, two subjects participated in the experiment at a time, one in each chamber. The buttons were so arranged that pressing the right-hand button in the first chamber gave the second player a point, while the left-hand button would deliver a shock to him. The second chamber was wired in a similar way, with the exception that the right-hand button delivered shock and the left provided points to the man in the first chamber. Using the matrix model outlined above, we can diagram the situation as in Fig. 4.2. The + indicates points and the − shock. It is immediately apparent that the

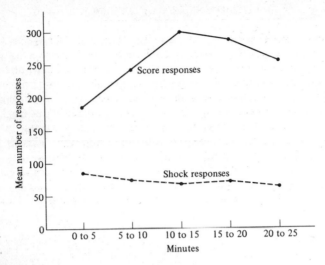

Fig. 4.3 Shock and score in a minimal social interchange. (Adapted from Sidowski, Wyckoff, and Tabory, 1956.)

optimum cell for mutual gain is that one in which individual *A* presses his right button and player *B* presses his left. The statement that this was a "conservative" test of the assumption stems from the fact that subjects were not specifically aware that the situation was a social one. They were not informed that there was another participant, and no communication was allowed between them.

The major interest of the study was, of course, the number of times the score buttons were pushed, as opposed to the shock buttons. Would subjects tend toward a relationship in which they were both receiving the maximal reward possible as a pair? The means for point and shock decisions can be found in Fig. 4.3. Here we find that the mean number of button pushes for points accelerated rapidly during the first 15 minutes and then essentially remained at the enhanced level. At the same time the shock choices underwent a slow, continuous decline. The difference between the two curves is statistically significant, and the increase in point pushes is also significant. In all fairness, it should be added that it did take a relatively large amount of shock to produce these results. When small amounts were used, little accommodation was found.

It may be concluded, however, that even when the "social" characteristics of the situation are at a bare minimum, there is a strong indication that over time persons tend to engage in behavior that provides the greatest mutual benefit.

THE IMPORTANCE OF SEQUENCE

In the matrix model sketched out above, each behavioral act of one individual was displayed in combination with each possible activity of a second person. Each combination was said to provide a certain amount of satisfaction or dissatisfaction to each individual. The formulation thus far, however, has allowed us to circumvent a most important issue, the issue of sequence. The major question here is whether we are able to make better predictions and improve our understanding by taking into account the *order* in which various activities are carried out over time. For example, one illustration we used earlier was the combination of A's aggression and B's passivity. If we were interested in predicting the subsequent behavior of each individual, it would make a considerable difference whether A's aggression was in response to B's submission, or B's submission was in response to A's aggression.

One of the clearest demonstrations of the importance of sequence occurred in an extension of the study just described. As you may recall, Sidowski and his colleagues allowed their subjects to press buttons at liberty in delivering outcomes to their partners. It was thus impossible to isolate any effects due to variation in sequence. A second group of investigators (Kelley, Thibaut, Radloff, and Mundy, 1962) viewed this as a major shortcoming. Initially, they reasoned that the best way to describe a subject's behavior in this minimal relationship was with the maxim, "win-stay, lose-change." That is, if a subject received points (won) by pressing a given button, he would continue to press it. If he was shocked as a result of pressing the button (lost), he would shift to the other button. Such an assumption is, of course, quite compatible with our earlier discussion of the maximization of gratification. However, this reasoning has very important implications when we turn to the matter of sequence.

Let us compare two possible sequences: the *simultaneous* and the *alternation*. In the former circumstance both members of a relationship are responding at the same time and without foreknowledge of the other's actions. One of the most poignant examples of this sequence is found in O'Henry's *The Gift of the Magi*. The impoverished young hero sacrifices his handsome watch in order to buy his beloved a set of tortoise shell combs for her long hair as a Christmas gift; at the same time, she purchases a chain worthy of his watch with money received from selling her hair. In the experimental scheme developed by Sidowski *et al.*, simultaneous responding is a simple matter to arrange. Both participants are required to press the button of their choice on a signal from the experimenter.

The alternation sequence is much more common in social relationships. In this case, A acts toward B, and B responds toward A, which response influences A's next action. You can easily discern what this would mean in an experimental context. On signal, one member would press a button,

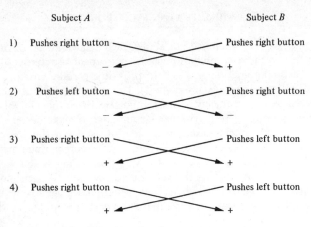

Fig. 4.4   The simultaneous sequence.

giving either reward or punishment to his partner; and on the subsequent signal, his partner would press a button delivering one of the two outcomes to him, and so on.

But what implications do these different sequences have for behavior in a minimal social situation? Let us see. The simultaneous sequence is outlined in Fig. 4.4. In this case, consider the possibility that at random both members first chose the right button. As you will recall, for person *A*, depressing this button would deliver a point to *B;* at the same time, *B* would deliver shock to *A*. If the "win-stay, lose-change" assumption is correct, during the second trial *A* should shift, having been shocked as a result of pushing the right button, and *B* should repeat his earlier decision. Thus, during the second trial, *A* should deliver shock to *B*, and *B* should also deliver shock to *A*. Inasmuch as both have now been punished, each should shift buttons, *A* pushing right and *B* left. As a result, both should then receive positive outcomes, and from then on, neither should change. In effect, if the "win-stay, lose-change" formulation is correct, simultaneous responding should ultimately lead to mutual benefit.

This state of affairs can be contrasted with the alternation pattern diagramed in Fig. 4.5. In this instance, the first stage might see *A* push the right button and thus deliver points to *B*. As in the simultaneous example, *B* first responds at random and, by choosing right, administers shock to *A*. Since *A* has thus received shock for a right choice on the second stage, he shifts and delivers shock to *B*. Since *B*'s right button has thus yielded shock, he shifts to the left and the result is a point for *A*. The third stage should thus see *A* remaining with the left button, *B* shocked, and *B* shifting right to administer shock to *A*. On the fourth round, *A* thus shifts right to reward *B*, and as a result, *B* stays right to punish *A*. If you look closely, you will see that stage four is essentially the same as the first stage. The theory would

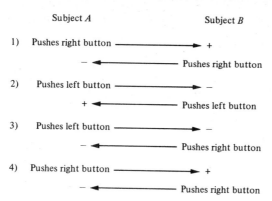

Fig. 4.5   The alternation sequence.

then predict that the entire sequence would continue to recycle. In the alternation condition, then, mutual benefit is much more difficult to achieve.

Of course it is possible that, by chance, partners in both situations might reward each other on the first trial, in which case there would be no changes. Or both could punish each other on the first trial, in which case both would shift to reward each other. In such cases the basic assumption would not differentiate between the two sequences. However, in comparing the two sequence conditions, such felicitous combinations should occur by chance with roughly equal frequency in both cases. The mutually defeating sequence in Fig. 4.5 should be confined to the simultaneous sequence condi-

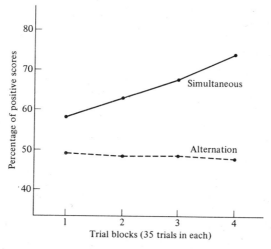

Fig. 4.6   Accommodation under two response sequences. (Adapted from Kelley, Thibaut, Radloff, and Mundy, 1962.)

tion alone. It thus becomes useful to test the difference between the two sequences experimentally, and this is precisely what Kelley and his colleagues did.

In an experimental situation that was much like that of Sidowski *et al.* (with the exception that humanism prevailed and subjects received more points for a + response, and lost points but were not shocked for the − responses), subjects produced over 140 trials. The results appear in Fig. 4.6. The findings clearly support the hypothesis: the simultaneous procedure was far superior in producing positive outcomes to the participants. The difference between the two conditions in number of rewards received by the members of the relationship is manifest in the first 35 trials, and steadily increases. In the simultaneous condition, partners enjoy an increasing number of positive outcomes; in the alternation condition, no progress whatsoever is made in increasing mutual benefits. The "win-stay, lose-change" version of the hedonic assumption accounts very well for the sequence differences.

OUTCOME SEQUENCE

The Kelley *et al.* study is a good demonstration of the importance of sequence in understanding accommodation in social relationships. While this is a good point to keep in mind in principle, you may quite well feel that in practice we have removed ourselves a good distance from ordinary social encounters. After all, in how many relationships does one find pure cases of simultaneous or alternation sequences? If we consider the problem of sequence in a different light, we can restore our faith in the relevance of such work to everyday life. The paramount problem we just faced was taking into account the order in which each participant responds to the other. The concern was thus with what might be termed the *sequence of responses*. The response sequence can be contrasted with the *sequence of outcomes*. Here the problem is to take into account the sequence of rewards and punishments that each participant in a relationship receives from the other over time.

If you looked closely at the data from the Kelley *et al.* study (Fig. 4.6), you probably realized that, even under the simultaneous condition, accommodation was a long time in developing. Even by the fourth block of 35 trials the level of positive outcomes had reached only 75%, while the "win-stay, lose-change" model outlined in Fig. 4.4 would have predicted perfect accommodation in at least four trials. In part, the reason for less than perfect accommodation in this situation can be attributed to the sequence of outcomes. That is, on any given trial the individual is responding to the *total pattern* of rewards and punishments up until that time. Although pushing the right button may elicit points on the fourth trial, the individual also knows that it elicited shock only three trials ago. In other words, the sequence of satisfaction or dissatisfaction over time is as important to take into account in understanding an ongoing relationship as is the order of response.

Some of the most engaging work dealing with outcome sequence effects has been carried out by Aronson and his associates (Aronson and Linder, 1965; Sigall and Aronson, 1967). Their research not only lends support to our argument, but sheds additional light on the problem of when satisfaction is not satisfying. (See pp. 23ff.) In addition, the broad relevance of the findings is quickly grasped.

The basic question with which Aronson's research was concerned was the satisfaction value of various sequences of positive as opposed to negative outcomes. Consider for a moment the following sequences:

1) +   +   +   +   —   —   —   —

2) +   +   +   +   —   —   —   —

3) —   —   —   —   +   +   +   +

4) —   —   —   —   —   —   —   —

With no other information provided, what combination of outcomes would you predict to be most preferred or satisfying, which least? A quick glance at the various combinations and a nod in the direction of elementary hedonistic principles might lead to the prediction that sequence (1) would be most preferred, (2) and (3) equally preferred, and (4) least preferred. After all, the greater the absolute number of positive outcomes, the more preferable is the sequence.

Aronson and his colleagues were unconvinced by this elementary line of reasoning. They were particularly concerned with those cases in which outcomes change over time. It seemed to them, for example, that in the — — — — + + + + sequence, negative outcomes would produce an initial state of dissatisfaction. However, when positive outcomes were eventually experienced, they would possess not only their intrinsic value, but an *additional* positive component attributable to the fact that they reduced or alleviated the earlier dissatisfaction. The person who provides approval after initial disapproval should thus be most appreciated. The authors draw sustenance in this speculation from Spinoza's *The Ethics,* in which the proposition is ventured that "Hatred which is completely vanquished by love passes into love; and love is thereupon greater than if hatred had not preceded it."

In the case of the + + + + — — — — sequence, the reverse of this proposition should obtain. Not only are the latter outcomes negative, but they also eradicate the earlier rewards and are thus the more to be disliked. As a result, the investigators were led to feel that the negative-to-positive sequence, although not producing so much ostensible reward as a continued positive sequence, should be most preferred. By the same token, the positive-to-negative sequence should be less preferred than the continuously negative one.

To test these assumptions, female undergraduates at the University of Minnesota were used. When a subject arrived for the study she was asked if she would help in conducting the experiment. Specifically it was her task to carry out short interviews through a one-way mirror with a second girl who was said to be an experimental subject in a verbal conditioning study. Part of the second girl's task was to form an impression of the person conducting the interview (the original subject). Thus, after each of the short conversations, the female undergraduate was confronted with what appeared to be a spontaneous reaction to her. In point of fact, these "spontaneous" reactions were quite carefully planned.

The so-called "subject in the verbal conditioning study" was a confederate of the experimenter whose impressions of the real subject (who thought all the while that she was helping to conduct the experiment) carefully conformed to one of the four standard sequence patterns. For example, in the negative-to-positive sequence the subject heard the interviewee describe her during the first three interviews as a "dull conversationalist," "a rather ordinary person," "not very intelligent," and so on. After the fourth conversation the impression was improved, and this enhanced impression continued to the end of the last interview. At this point the subject heard herself described as a person who was "extremely interesting" and "likable." For the other conditions of the experiment, precisely the same reactions to the subject were used; only the sequences were altered.

The major dependent variable in this first study (Aronson and Linder, 1965) was the subject's attraction to the person she had heard evaluate her. Parenthetically, it should be noted that in the social exchange framework a close relationship is assumed between attraction and satisfaction. Attraction ratings are considered a verbalized indicator of the state of satisfaction or dissatisfaction produced by the behavior of the other. In this case, subjects rated their evaluator on such dimensions as "friendliness," "warmth," "intelligence," and so on, and all ratings were summed. The mean attraction ratings for the various conditions can be found in the left-hand column of Table 4.1. As you can see, the results clearly support the preliminary reasoning. The negative-to-positive sequence engenders the greatest amount of attraction, the positive-to-negative the least. Statistical tests further showed that the negative-to-positive sequence produced significantly greater attraction than the positive-to-positive. The positive-to-positive was significantly greater than the negative-to-negative, and the latter differed significantly from the positive-to-negative condition.

You may retain some doubt, of course, as to whether attraction ratings are a valid indicator of the satisfaction which another has provided. We would be on much safer grounds if it could be shown that attraction in this type of situation is accompanied by the desire to provide the other with positive outcomes in return. A second study (Sigall and Aronson, 1967),

TABLE 4.1

Attraction and Conformity Means
Under Varying Reaction Sequences

	Attraction Rating	Opinion Conformity
1) Negative-Positive	+ 7.67	4.67
2) Positive-Positive	+ 6.42	3.58
3) Negative-Negative	+ 2.52	3.00
4) Positive-Negative	+ 0.87	2.83

conducted along similar lines to the first, provided the needed reassurances. The dependent variable in this investigation was the degree to which the subject would agree with the opinions of the person who had rated her. Opinion conformity provides an indication, then, of what the subject is willing to do for the other. The mean conformity scores can also be found in Table 4.1. As we observe, the pattern of findings is in marked agreement with the attraction ratings of the initial study. The statistical results are not quite so compelling, but the similarity in pattern is striking.

Although these results are certainly interesting enough, you may yet share with many psychologists a certain degree of uneasiness about them. Although the "gain through triumph over loss" rationale makes good sense when applied to the comparison of the negative-to-positive with the positive-to-negative conditions, the theory is a little less clear in explaining why the negative-to-positive sequence should be responded to more favorably than the positive-to-positive. Nor does the rationale explain why the positive-to-negative sequence should be reacted to less favorably than the continuous negative expressions. Continuous positive ratings from the other are no doubt rewarding; it is not clear why the rewards received from the *replacement* of negatives by positives should be greater. These results are in need of a more elaborate explanation.

Possibly your reaction to this puzzle has been to think back to the Gewirtz and Baer study on the satiation of social approval. However, a satiation explanation of why continuous positive ratings did not elicit greater liking also seems remote. One would be hard put in the present study to argue that the eight brief reactions to the subject exceeded some optimum state.

More reasonable is the possibility that the continuous positive appraisal really did little to fulfill learned needs for social approval, nor did continuous negative appraisal vitally frustrate such needs. Why? Because in order for social approval to have an impact, it must be *personalistic* in character (Gergen, 1965). It must appear to be contingent on one's own behavior. If another's regard for you is not dependent on your behavior, it becomes impersonal and irrelevant to your feelings of esteem. Continuous positive appraisals often have this character. If the person who is providing them seems not to be reacting or responding to behavior which you as a person are emitting, they lose their significance as indicators of worth. Rather, they appear to be built into the other person's style of behavior—his personality— as in the stereotype we have of the superficial charm of the Southern Belle.

In this context, subjects who first experienced negative appraisals and then positive are in an optimum position. Since these subjects received different appraisals for various behaviors on their part, the positive appraisals appear to be directed at them personally. As a result, the positive appraisals may have greater satisfaction value. The same reasoning would also apply in the positive-to-negative vs. the negative-to-negative condition. Continuous negative appraisals may appear to be impersonal, while the change in the other's ratings over time must have appeared to be in reaction to the subjects themselves.

In spite of the difficulty in pinpointing a necessary and sufficient explanation, your mind may be spinning with the implication of the results. The study suggests, for example, that the best way to lose a close friend or romantic partner may be to provide continuous and undifferentiated positive outcomes. To love with complete enthusiasm may undermine the relationship; the constant lover may soon be the lover pale and wan. In the area of leadership, the leader with the most devoted followers may well be the one who has cracked the whip at the outset and slowly warmed up over time.

THE HIDDEN ASSUMPTIONS

During the development of these various arguments, an entire series of assumptions has crept in, and has probably been accepted without question. With our commitment to the "code of good practices" laid out in Chapter One, we should try to guard ourselves against the unexamined and unsupported assumption. What has inserted itself into our theorizing in such a surreptitious fashion? Specifically, a set of assumptions of a very pernicious variety—those dealing with internal and unobservable processes. In effect, we have admitted into our theory a set of concepts that refer not to real-world entities, but to hypothetical processes or events within the individual. Before moving on to the study of interpersonal bargaining, we should stop briefly to identify the concepts we have accepted into the arena, and satisfy ourselves that we wish them to remain.

Confessing that we may even now fail to recognize some assumptions because of our deep immersion in the ideology of Western culture, attention does need to be given to the following:

1. Data exchange and retrieval. As you will recall, the studies of sequence carried out by Aronson and his associates were used to demonstrate the effects of the sequence of outcomes. It was pointed out that any response to a person was dependent not only on his behavior at the moment, but also on the sequence of behavior toward us in the past. In order to accept this point, it is also necessary to accept the proposition that persons store information gathered from the environment and are capable of retrieving it at some later date. We are so accustomed to accepting the notion of memory and using it as an explanatory device that this assumption could easily creep in unnoticed. However, the assumption appears sufficiently useful in the present theory, as well as in real life, that it appears eminently worth retaining.

2. Comparison process. We have already assumed that people are capable of "experiencing" positive or negative outcomes—of having hedonic reactions. However, studies such as those of Aronson *et al.* indicate that people are also capable of recognizing the *difference* between these outcomes. That is, they are able to consider two or more pieces of information at the same time and *compare* them on a hedonic level. They are capable of distinguishing that *A* is better or worse than *B.* Again, common experience overwhelmingly supports this assumption. We should not assume, on the other hand, that such a process operates in a straightforward manner. Other research suggests that outcomes roughly resembling each other may be *assimilated*—treated as equivalent—while those which are discrepant may be *contrasted*—seen as more discrepant than they really are (Sherif, Sherif, and Nebergall, 1965). In addition, research on cognitive dissonance (cf. Brehm, 1956) indicates that one's comparison may vitally be affected by what he possesses, as opposed to what he is without—a "sour grapes" phenomenon. Such work must ultimately be integrated into the exchange framework.

3. Logical processes. If we look closely at the research on accommodation in a minimal relationship, it also seems clear that we must accept the capacity for persons to perform cognitive operations on the information available to them—to go from particular facts to general conclusions, and from general statements to particular facts. In essence, without the ability to reason both inductively and deductively, it would be impossible to achieve accommodation. Again we have added a useful hypothetical construct. But again, to assume that it operates in a simplex fashion would be a mistake. The literature is rife with examples of logical thinking gone awry. Until the process of thinking is understood, we shall never be able fully to penetrate the exchange process—a point that will become quite evident in the following chapter on interpersonal bargaining.

REFERENCES

Aronson, E., and D. Linder, Gain and loss of esteem as determinants of interpersonal attractiveness. *Journal of Experimental Social Psychology,* **1,** 156-172, 1965.

Blau, P. M., *Exchange and Power in Social Life*. New York: John Wiley and Sons, 1964.

Brehm, J., Post-decision changes in the desirability of alternatives. *Journal of Abnormal and Social Psychology*, 52, 384-389, 1956.

Gergen, K. J., The effects of interaction goals and personalistic feedback on the presentation of self. *Journal of Personality and Social Psychology*, 1, 413-424, 1965.

Homans, G. C., *Social Behavior: Its Elementary Forms*. New York: Harcourt, Brace, and World, 1961.

Kelley, H. H., Interpersonal accommodation. *American Psychologist*, 23, 399-410, 1968.

Kelley, H. H., J. W. Thibaut, R. Radloff, and D. Mundy, The development of cooperation in the "minimal social situation." *Psychological Monographs*, 76, No. 19, Whole No. 538, 1962.

Sears, R. R., A theoretical framework for personality and social behavior. *American Psychologist*, 6, 476-484, 1951.

Sherif, C. W., M. Sherif, and R. E. Nebergall, *Attitude and Attitude Change*. Philadelphia: W. B. Saunders, 1965.

Sidowski, J. B., L. B. Wyckoff, and L. Tabory, The influence of reinforcement and punishment in a minimal social situation. *Journal of Abnormal and Social Psychology*, 52, 115-119, 1956.

Sigall, H., and E. Aronson, Opinion change and the gain-loss model of interpersonal attraction. *Journal of Experimental Social Psychology*, 3, 178-188, 1967.

Thibaut, J. W., and H. H. Kelley, *The Social Psychology of Groups*. New York: John Wiley and Sons, 1959.

CHAPTER FIVE

The Psychology of Interpersonal Bargaining

As we have seen, experiments dealing with exchange under minimal social conditions can be very useful. They allow us to break through the multiple complexities of everyday relationships and deal with one or two essentials at a time, under controlled and standardized circumstances. In this way the investigator can deal directly with basic assumptions. But how far can one generalize the findings of such studies? The problem of the extent to which one can generalize from the findings of laboratory experiments is a complex one and common to all sciences. The particular issue at stake here, however, has to do with the validity of basic assumptions as one adds greater and greater complexity to the situation. We cannot always remain on the level of minimal relations. Continued progress must be made toward catching the full-blown relationship in our theoretical nets. The research to be discussed in this chapter on what has been termed *interpersonal bargaining* represents a second significant step in this direction. What new issues does such research raise? In what ways must we expand our conceptual framework?

MATRIX CONFIGURATIONS

At the outset it is important to recognize the limited nature of the payoff matrix used in research in minimal relationships as we have discussed it thus far. In matrix form, the configuration of payoffs in these relationships can be illustrated as in Fig. 5.1.

The figure indicates that A's choice of a_1 always provides points for B, while a_2 produces shock for B. Similarly, b_1 and b_2 deliver reward or punishment to A.

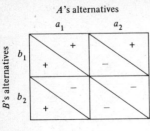

Figure 5.1

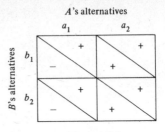

Figure 5.2

However, this particular matrix is only one of a large number of possibilities. Consider, for example, Fig. 5.2. In this relationship, A is clearly in an optimal position. Whatever behavior B engages in produces reward for A. At the same time, A can choose to reward or punish B as he desires. Behavior a_1 will always punish B, while a choice of a_2 may bring satisfaction to B. Thibaut and Kelley (1959) have used the term *fate control* to refer to this particular configuration. In essence, A has absolute control over the fate of B, and B is unable to exert any influence over what he receives from A. Regardless of his decision, A is always rewarded.

For anyone interested in political structure or social power, this type of configuration should begin to stimulate a good deal of thought. Many theorists have attempted to define social power, but the problem of precision or of making these definitions operational has been a major one. From the present vantage point, power can be defined as the relative capacity of one person to affect the outcomes or satisfactions of another. Fate control as represented above provides absolute power for A over B. As you can see, the exchange framework would lend itself quite well to systematizing and conceptualizing various forms of social power as they exist in the real world. Studies using such configurations thus present the possibility of shedding light on behavior in political systems.

But let us move on to compare the fate control matrix with Fig. 5.3. In this case, A cannot be affected by B, but he does have substantially less control over B than in the above situation. To be sure, B can only reward A. However, A's decision of a_1 or a_2 does not necessarily mean that B will be rewarded or punished. The term *behavior control* has been used to describe this case, pointing up the fact that changes in A's behavior make certain options more or less desirable for B. If A chooses a_1, B is *influenced* to choose b_1 if he desires reward. To continue our analogy of political structure, the behavior control matrix might be likened to the tax structure. The government is assured of obtaining a portion of your income, but what it chooses to tax may have a direct influence on your behavior. Perhaps it is diagnostic of our culture that very high taxes are currently levied on activities that have a pleasurable component. High taxes on gifts, alcohol, cigarettes, and gasoline, for example, all have the effect of altering behavior in the ascetic direction.

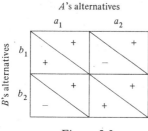

Figure 5.3

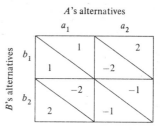

Figure 5.4

These particular matrices are only a few out of a vast number that could be generated in a two-person, two-choice situation. In fact, with just the simple 2 × 2 matrix, one can form as many as 256 different patterns of joint payoffs, and each pattern probably has its counterpart in everyday life. This is not to say that research has been carried out comparing behavior of persons in all these various conditions. On the contrary, little has been done in the way of comparative work. Why? The major reason is that the gross payoffs symbolized by + and − are too imprecise. Investigators have found that it is possible to convert these gross payoffs into quantifiable units. Instead of all +'s being equal, some might be worth more than others (e.g., +4 > +2). In economic terms, not all +'s have the same utility. And what is more important, as soon as one is dealing in relative degrees of reward or punishment (a situation much more analogous to real life), new issues and complexities begin to emerge. This latter point will be amplified in the following section.

BARGAINING AND THE PRISONERS' DILEMMA

Much was said in the last chapter about interpersonal accommodation, or that process by which both members of a relationship migrate toward maximizing joint returns. What new ingredients are added to the problem of accommodation when numerical weights are assigned to payoffs? In this section we shall take a single example and discuss it in detail. The choice of example is not an arbitrary one. As it turns out, this single problem has created more research interest than any other in the area.

Let us first take the matrix used in the minimal social exchange work, and add a set of numerical weights. Both the original matrix and assigned weights appear in Fig. 5.4. What has happened? In this particular case, a dilemma of profound proportions has been created. The choice combination yielding greatest mutual benefit is $a_1 b_1$. However, by choosing these alternatives, each person gives up the possibility of twice as much benefit if he had chosen to gain at the expense of the other. At the same time, if we assume simultaneous responding, opting for mutual benefit runs the risk of being exploited by the other—of losing while the other profits. And, should both partners choose to exploit, the result is mutual catastrophe.

By converting gross payoffs to numerical form we have, in this particular case, created a multifaceted conflict. In the early case, if each participant attempted to maximize his own gain, the result was maximum joint gain. However, in this case, to maximize one's own gain is to minimize one's partner's gain. Thus, the maximization of own gain has been viewed as the *competitive* choice. The maximization of joint gain involves forgoing complete self-seeking for a common good; this choice is termed *cooperative*. In a sense, these motives are pitted against each other, and the situation is thus said to be one where *mixed motives* prevail. This view is oversimplified, however, in that a competitive choice runs the risk of loss should the other also choose competitively, and a cooperative choice leaves one open to being exploited. Thus, fear of the other may influence one's choice.

This particular conflict has been called the "prisoners' dilemma," a term stemming from the following situation: Two men are suspected of having committed a crime together. They are placed in separate cells and each is informed separately that he may choose to confess or not, subject to the following stipulations: (1) if both independently choose not to confess, they will receive only moderate punishment (condition a_1b_1 in Fig. 5.4); (2) on the other hand, if one chooses not to confess, and the other simultaneously confesses, the confessor will receive the minimal sentence while his partner will be given the maximal sentence (a_1b_2 or a_2b_1); (3) if both choose to confess, they will both be given heavy sentences (a_2b_2). Thus, both confession and nonconfession can yield rewards, but each has its attendant pitfalls.

Interestingly enough, this same problem is one that has traversed disciplinary grounds to engage not only psychologists, but economists and mathematicians as well. For the economist, the dilemma is one that pits exploitation for profit against cooperation for mutual gain. For the mathematician the more general theory of games could be brought to bear, with the prisoners' dilemma viewed as one of the more interesting of the two-person, nonzero-sum games (a zero-sum game being one in which either player's gain must entail an equal amount of loss for the opponent). The classic work joining economic and mathematical interests in this and related problems is Von Neumann and Morgenstern's *Theory of Games and Economic Behavior*, published in 1944. Psychologists began to be intrigued with such problems on several counts. For one, it was clear that the optimum behavior prescribed by the rational dictates of game theory was typically not the behavior in which people engaged. In essence, the red flag was waved for many psychologists when people proved to act less than rationally. The strictly rational choice, however, is also the exploitative one in most such dilemmas. Thus, psychologists with a humanistic bent also became intrigued. Why would people choose to exploit rather than cooperate?

There were even broader reasons for the social psychologist to be interested in the prisoners' dilemma. Social psychologists have long been intrigued with the question of how persons come to create the stable patterns of give and take that we call organized society. From both the Darwinian and Freudian viewpoints, man is viewed as basically a brutish animal who seeks his own gratification regardless of others' suffering. In raw form, man would appear to be an exploitative creature. How is it, then, that organized society can exist? How is it that men everywhere forgo self-interest and work for the common good? Those of you who are interested in political philosophy will no doubt recognize this as the same problem to which Thomas Hobbes addressed himself in *The Leviathan,* and which led to the concept of the social contract. For the social psychologist, the prisoners' dilemma seemed to be a way of studying at close range a process that may form the basis for organized society.

Again the implications are far outrunning the actual state of fact. What is required at this point is an examination of the research enterprise and what light it has been able to shed thus far.

DETERMINANTS OF BEHAVIOR IN THE PRISONERS' DILEMMA

Research on the prisoners' dilemma is highly beneficial to our task of theory building. Such research begins to differentiate more finely among the various payoffs in a situation, and to show how people behave when there is more than one motive at stake. In addition, it demonstrates the increasing number of variables that must be taken into account as we move from simple to more complex social relationships. Let us first examine some of the most important determining variables, and then turn to the issue of the adequacy of the research.

The Payoff Matrix

At the outset there seemed little reason to suspect that people would be guided in their decisions by any factors other than the payoffs provided in the matrix. People would choose, it was reasoned, in such a way as to maximize the chance for gain and minimize the chance for loss. This orientation toward bargaining has been called by mathematical game theorists the *minimax strategy.* As you can readily discern, the concept of minimax has its basis in classic theories of hedonism discussed earlier. But do people generally follow the minimax strategy as dictated by the matrix? To what extent are their decisions dominated by the matrix configuration?

To explore these and other questions, Minas, Scodel, Marlowe, and Rawson (1960) had undergraduate men and women at Ohio State participate in a study in which each subject was placed behind a partition. In front of him was a payoff matrix and two buttons, one red and the other black. It was explained to the subject that his partner (whom he could neither see nor communicate with) was faced with a similar arrangement. They could win pennies as indicated by the payoff matrix, depending on what combina-

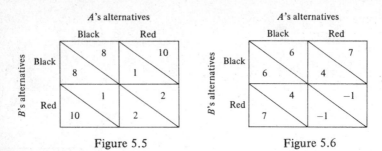

Figure 5.5   Figure 5.6

tion of buttons was pressed on any trial. Thus, in the matrix of Fig. 5.5, a red choice by each of the two participants would net each of them two cents, a black choice by both on the same trial would yield eight cents for each, and so on. The "opponent's" choice and the payoff were shown to each of the participants at the end of each trial.

Before looking at the results, you might first have a friend play the game with you. You can use coins, with "heads" denoting a red choice and "tails" a black. At a given signal, each of you should publicly show "heads" or "tails," and then jot down the winnings on that trial. Without communicating about why you chose as you did on each trial, or otherwise attempting to influence your friend, try to keep a record of the percentage of red choices over, let's say, 30 trials. After 30 trials tally up the number of red choices made by you and your partner and convert these numbers to the percentage of red choices of the 60 choices that were made.

Now that you have tried the experience you are in a better position to see what the Ohio State students did in this type of situation. First we might ask what the minimax strategy is for this matrix. A quick scanning of the matrix should reveal that the solution is to push the red button or to show "heads," as the case may be. The red choice will allow you to win the greatest number of points (10 as opposed to 8) should your partner choose black, and to minimize your losses (2 as opposed to 1) should your partner choose red. But on what percentage of the trials did you and your partner choose red? If my guess is correct, and you are like most people who participate in such procedures, you chose red, the rational choice, a good deal less than 100% of the time. In the Minas *et al.* study, 62% of the choices made by subjects were red. (Surprisingly, males and females exploited in roughly equal amounts.) It is evident, then, that the matrix does not completely dictate decision making.

This is not to say, however, that the matrix has no effect. A true test of matrix effects would require that different groups of subjects confront different forms of the matrix and their scores be compared. Additional subjects were thus run in the modification of the prisoners' dilemma shown in Fig. 5.6. In this case, as you can see, one maximizes winnings by choosing red (7 as opposed to 6), but the chances for loss are also greater (−1 for red, as opposed to +4 for black). In this particular set of circumstances, subjects' red choices drop to 50%. Clearly, the configuration of payoffs does have an effect.

That peoples' choices should be influenced by the prospects of material gain is not overly surprising. However, the more intriguing question is why their choices in the present case were not completely dictated by the matrix. Why were the actions "nonrational" from a game-theoretical point of view? In the first matrix one might answer by saying that the red choice, while rational, was also the exploitative one. Since there is a negative value (dissatisfaction) attached to thoroughgoing exploitation in our society, red choices were made less than 100% of the time. However compelling, this reasoning cannot explain the results for the second of the two matrices shown above. In this case the minimax solution is actually black, a coopera-tive choice. And yet subjects chose to cooperate only some 50% of the time. Here one could indeed argue that one receives satisfaction from exploiting others. Having a sense for the dramatic, Minas and his colleagues leaned toward this latter view. It was their opinion that subjects first wish to obtain money. However, once a certain amount of capital has been accumulated, their major aim is to achieve *more* money than their partner. Instead of maximizing gain, they wish to maximize the *differences* between themselves and their partner. The investigators found some support for their specula-tions in the fact that across a wide variety of matrices, subjects tend to increase the amount of exploitation as the game proceeds.

Whatever the psychological gains are, it is apparent that there is not a one-to-one relationship between the gains and losses represented in the matrix and satisfaction and dissatisfaction at the psychological level. This is not to say that the minimax strategy does not prevail for most people. Rather, it is to say that the payoffs or the utilities for various actions are not all represented in the matrix. Social motives or satisfactions must also be figured into the minimax principle. Thus far we have faced the possibility that cultural values assigned to exploitation may play a part. But what other factors have been shown to influence bargaining behavior?

Interaction Goals

In thinking over the various sources of potential reward in the bargaining situation, it soon becomes apparent that we must account for the particular goals or motives of the participants. In any dyad, each of the parties seeks rewards from the relationship. We may want nurturance and financial sup-port from a parent but intellectual stimulation and challenge from a teacher. The effect of changing interaction goals is to alter the utilities of various entries in the matrix. If one's major goal is to gain the friendship of the other, then the cost of choosing to exploit is greatly enhanced; not only may you end up in a low-outcome stalemate $(a_2 b_2)$, but at the same time you may lose the other's friendship.

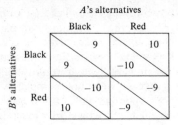

Figure 5.7

Perhaps the clearest exposition of this point was made by Deutsch (1960a). In this case the effects of three different goals or motivational stances were compared. Prior to the bargaining procedure, each subject received instructions to approach the relationship in one of the following ways:

1. Cooperatively: the subject was told to take an interest in his partner's welfare as well as his own, to consider his partner's winnings, losses, and personal feelings.

2. Individualistically: winning as much money as possible for self, without any concern for how much the other participant won or lost, was said to be the sole aim.

3. Competitively: while making money was to be viewed as important, making more money than the opponent was said to be the primary goal.

The matrix used in this investigation is an intriguing one inasmuch as it places such a strong emphasis on interpersonal trust. (See Fig. 5.7.) To distrust the other person or to attempt to exploit him is to risk great loss. Major gains are possible only when both partners are willing to trust each other to cooperate. You can possibly see the parallel between this situation and peace negotiations involved in both the wars over Korea and Vietnam. Unilateral withdrawal, disarmament, or curtailment of hostile activity (a_1) also places one in the position of military jeopardy (a_1b_1). To continue hostilities (b_2), however, would most certainly mean continued bloodshed (a_2b_2) for both sides.

Unfortunately, the game itself was played for only one trial. If the game had been extended, it would have been possible to assess the reactions of the other to the strategies employed under these three motivational sets. And the strategies did prove to be markedly different. Subjects motivated to be cooperative were generally about 50% more cooperative than those attempting to be individualistic. And the latter were roughly 20% more cooperative than subjects motivated to be competitive. It should be noted, however, that within the same experiment the choice sequence was also varied. Under conditions in which subjects were allowed to alter their choice after seeing the choice of their partner, and to do this continuously until agreement was reached, cooperation was maximal in all three conditions of motivation.

Characteristics of the Other and of the Context

While the goals of the participants are clearly of great importance, the bargaining relationship may also be viewed in broader perspective. As you may recall, one advantage of bargaining research is that it separates out for study a specific subsection of the larger interaction matrix that might characterize a more full-blown relationship. However, there are many who feel that bargaining research has not been totally successful in this attempt, and that even within the confines of the experimental laboratory, subjects consider their relationship to each other in broader terms than the simple matrix suggests. From this point of view, the experimental game represents only one aspect of the relationship between subjects. Subjects may feel their game behavior has implications for their relationship outside the experiment, and their earlier relationships may also dictate their choices in the experiment.

Thus, the characteristics of one's partner in the experiment, and the characteristics of the more general context surrounding the experiment, should both have implications for bargaining behavior. And certainly this view is more compatible with "bargaining" as it takes place in daily life. In exchanging outcomes with others, we are constantly aware of the identity of each and the situation in which we find ourselves with them. A male reacts differently to an attractive than to an unattractive female, and differently with each depending on whether the context is a classroom or a lover's lane. But how could one go about incorporating such factors into the laboratory study of interpersonal bargaining? Marlowe, Gergen, and Doob (1966) attempted to answer this question, while at the same time trying to shed light on a more general hypothesis about social interaction.

The specific interest of the study was the effects on exploitative behavior of (1) differences in the perceived egotism of the other person and (2) variations in the amount of expected interaction. Initially it seemed that another who is egotistical can often be a threat to one's power in a situation. His display of superiority tends to minimize one's own abilities and threatens one's options for choice. It was thus felt that in a bargaining situation, subjects would attempt to reduce this potential imbalance in power by exploiting the person who appeared to be egotistical. In this way one could communicate his refusal to be taken advantage of. But what of the interaction context? How could this augment one's reaction to egotism? The one aspect of the context that seemed crucial in this case was the degree to which it provided longevity to the relationship. The necessity for reducing threat to one's own power seemed much enhanced when a long-term relationship was anticipated. If the interchange was limited only to the bargaining, the other would be less threatening to one's power.

It was thus predicted that when a further relationship is anticipated, a person bargaining with another who is perceived to be egotistical will be more exploitative than when no future interaction is expected.

With the humble, self-effacing character a different set of issues presents itself. Such a person, it was felt, often evokes feelings of pity, and to exploit him would most likely create feelings of guilt (a negative payoff). Such feelings should be particularly salient when one expects future interaction and a relationship in which the fact of the exploitation would always stand between the partners. At the same time, the humble person invites exploitation. In displaying his shortcomings, he lays himself open to the other's advantage. The appeal of exploitation should be especially salient when one does not subsequently have to meet the other face to face. It was hypothesized, then, that when another is perceived to be humble, he will be exploited more when one does not expect to interact with him than when he expects a relationship. Much the same reasoning can be brought to bear on the problem of warfare in the modern age. With some justification it has been said that we are in much greater danger of world war in the present than ever before. It is now possible to destroy entire cities from a remote and impersonal position behind a rocket control panel. In earlier times, killing necessitated a much closer relationship between aggressor and victim.

To test these predictions, Harvard freshmen were first asked to fill out a number of self-rating measures. They were then told that in order to have some impression of their partner in a decision task to follow, they would each be allowed to see their partner's self-ratings. At this point each subject received one of two specially prepared personality sketches. Half found their "partner" was a self-avowed world beater. He rated himself as extremely "clear thinking," "efficient," "confident," and so on. The remaining subjects received a questionnaire that suggested that their partner was just the opposite. He saw himself as "fuzzy-minded," "ineffective," and "lacking in self-confidence."

After this manipulation of perceived egotism, subjects were introduced to a bargaining situation with a standard prisoners' dilemma format. Before the actual bargaining procedure began, however, half the subjects in each of the above conditions were told that they would be able to meet their partner after the task had been completed and discuss their various decisions. Since all subjects were classmates, the implication was that their bargaining behavior could potentially affect any relationship between them for as long as three years. The other half of the subjects were told that they would never meet or learn the identity of the person with whom they worked on the task. These instructions constituted the manipulation of anticipated interaction. The game itself was 30 trials in duration, and all subjects were exposed to a 70% cooperative pattern of choices from their supposed partner.

The major dependent measure was, of course, the number of exploitative choices made by subjects in the various conditions. The mean numbers of red choices for subjects in the various conditions are graphed in Fig. 5.8. The results nicely substantiate the hypotheses. When bargaining with the egotist, subjects exploited him much more when they felt they would have

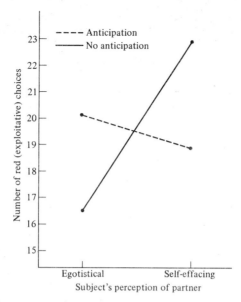

Fig. 5.8 Exploitation as a function of the other's personality and expectation of interaction. (From Marlowe, Gergen, and Doob, 1966. Copyright 1966 by the American Psychological Association, and reproduced by permission.)

to confront him personally than when they didn't expect a further relationship. When dealing with the humble person, exactly the reverse was found: greater exploitation when no further interaction was pending. As a commentary on human relationships, these latter results are perhaps the most unsettling. These subjects were faced with a person who prostrated himself before them, and who, during the bargaining procedure, made a cooperative decision on 21 of the 30 trials. In this situation, where anonymity was guaranteed, subjects were less cooperative than in any other condition, and exploited their partner on an average of 23 of the 30 trials. Surveillance and public exposure may indeed be very important factors in maintaining the cohesion of society.

The Other's Bargaining Behavior

One obvious factor that should influence a person's bargaining behavior is the behavior of his opponent (or partner, depending on how he construes the situation). If the other demonstrates a continuously exploitative approach, one might well react aggressively and exploit in return. However, if the choices of the other are demonstrably cooperative, one might be less inclined to exploit in return—that is, if he began to feel guilty over exploiting the other's overtures to peace and tranquillity.

In spite of the obviousness of this factor, there is little research to support the supposition. One reason for this is that most investigators allow the partners to play at will; in few instances do they insert "fake" decisions into the procedure. While maintaining the spontaneous character of the game, not taking control of this aspect of the stimulus to which subjects are exposed does permit a number of random factors to reduce the clarity of the results. But what happens when the partner's decisions are varied systematically? To explore this question Gergen and Goethals (unpublished) exposed subjects to a partner who chose cooperatively either 20% of the time (at random), 50% of the time, or in 80% of the trials. The game was 30 trials in length, and the matrix was identical to that used in the Marlowe *et al.* study described above. The effects were devastating, at least to our theory and hopes for humankind. Subjects' behavior was not affected in the slightest. They exploited the other approximately 65% of the time, regardless of his behavior. Most disappointingly, they tended to exploit him even when he showed marked tendencies toward cooperation. Does turning the other cheek ever pay? Perhaps, but it may take much more drastic amounts of cooperation than used in this case.

Individual Differences

After our discussion of individual variations in need for social approval (see pp. 25-28), it should come as no surprise that there are important individual differences in the tendency of people to exploit each other in the prisoners' dilemma situations. By virtue of their past history there are persons who have developed particular needs, or who gain satisfaction through particular styles of behavior. By developing measures of these styles, one can predict more precisely the behavior of any individual in the bargaining arena. By and large, these particular payoffs can be viewed as intrinsic (see p. 37). If external payoffs are held constant, it can be said that there are those who derive more internal satisfaction from being exploitative (or cooperative, as the case may be) than others. There are numerous studies that demonstrate the existence of such differences, and with the use of various measuring devices reliable predictions have been made of the degree to which a given person will take advantage of another.

One of the more interesting examples of this line of research was published by Deutsch in 1960 (Deutsch, 1960b), and stemmed from the longstanding interest social psychologists have had in the problem of racial prejudice. Adorno, Frenkel-Brunswik, Levinson, and Sanford had argued in 1950 that personality was all-important in determining what individuals were prone to intolerance. In particular, they argued that the dimension of authoritarianism was crucial to understanding racial prejudice. In general, the authoritarian syndrome was said to consist of anti-Semitic and anti-democratic attitudes, political and economic conservatism, and ethnocentrism.

In this particular study, the *F* scale (the most widely researched measure of authoritarianism, and particularly its ethnocentric character) was administered to subjects prior to the bargaining procedure. A prisoners' dilemma format was used, and subjects were placed in each of two situations. First, they were required to commit themselves to a choice that would be announced to their partner *before* the partner had to make his choice. In this case, to choose cooperatively would demonstrate great trust, because it allowed the other to take full advantage in his choice that followed. In the second condition, the shoe was on the other foot. Subjects were allowed to make their decision *after* they knew what their partner had decided. All subjects were told that their partner had made the trusting decision. This meant, of course, that the supposed partner was in a position to be exploited and their trust was on trial. Subjects were then allowed to make their decisions. The interests of this study were twofold: first, to assess the relationship between authoritarianism and trust of the partner; and second, to examine whether authoritarians were less trustworthy than nonauthoritarians. The results lent good support to the liberal ideology. Persons who were high on the authoritarian indicator were, first of all, less trusting; they were less likely to choose cooperatively, presumably because they felt they would be exploited if they did so. Second, they were also less trustworthy, and exploited their partner when he had chosen to cooperate. Both taking a chance on cooperation and cooperating with one who had placed his trust in them were alien to the authoritarians.

Interaction goals, characteristics of the other, the interaction context, and individual differences all serve as nonmatrix factors that influence bargaining behavior. While this list is hardly exhaustive, these factors do furnish some of the major sources of variation. It should also be realized that the end point of such studies is not to understand bargaining behavior *per se,* but to shed light on behavioral exchange in the everyday world. Thus, in this broader perspective, the various factors just discussed are ones that must be taken into account in understanding any ongoing relationship. Having raised the issue of broad perspective, we are now in a position to step back from the data and ask how successful bargaining research has been. Once we have made the assessment, we may finally turn to a study that has attempted to cope with some of the problems of traditional bargaining research and to open new vistas.

RESEARCH ON BARGAINING: HOW SUCCESSFUL?

As you may have realized, research on bargaining has a way of generating interest over and above its real-world relevance. The degree to which people act nonrationally, or the extent to which they will exploit each other under various conditions, can be very intriguing in and of itself. The methodology is also attractive in many respects. The conditions of any experiment are easily reproduced from one laboratory to another; endless variations can be made in the form of the matrix; the behavior of the participants is easily recorded. And too, results of various studies do have important implications for real world issues.

We spoke earlier of the problem of social organization and the development of prohibitions against an every-man-for-himself mentality. In the work we have reviewed thus far, we have learned that even when the payoffs for exploitation are high and the exploitative choice is rational, college students will not always choose to exploit. On the other hand, neither will they always cooperate when cooperation is the logical choice. As payoffs for exploitation change, so does the level of exploitation. Both cooperation and exploitation are also highly subject to the momentary motives operating within the situation. And we have further seen that the characteristics of the other person and the context may influence the degree of exploitation. People will not hesitate to take advantage of a humble person when they do not have to meet him. Finally, we were apprised of the fact that we might expect, both within and across cultures, wide variations in tendency toward exploitation. And though we might not be willing to leap from the laboratory to apply our data to national policy, certainly these various findings raise provocative questions which deserve close attention in the policy-making context. Yet, in spite of these many advantages, important difficulties remain. These now deserve our attention:

1. Ambiguity of the dependent variable. Investigators have often displayed a good deal of ingenuity in altering the conditions under which participants may bargain. The effects of a great many different variables have been gauged. On the other hand, the dominant focus of all this activity has been on a single, constricted behavioral act: whether the person chooses to do *a* or *b* (e.g., push a red or black button, push a switch to the right or the left). Most investigators are wont to assume that one of these choices is pro-social or cooperative in nature while the other belies the person's desire to exploit. However, such an assumption is not clearly justified. The cooperative choice may imply that the person desires to maximize joint gain; on the other hand, it may also indicate that he is not fearful of being exploited. In the same way, making the exploitative choice may be an attempt to ensure greater rewards for self than for the other, or, on the other hand, may be derived from a suspicion of the other's untrustworthy nature. A cooperative choice can be used by the subject to secure friendship and have nothing to do with the payoffs displayed in the matrix, and an exploitative choice may in fact be a way of expressing hostility. Research by Christie, Gergen, and Marlowe (1969) suggests that the exploitative choice is often used to punish the other's tendency to exploit and to signal him that cooperation is the only proper goal. In essence, the psychological meaning of pushing a red or black button is fraught with ambiguity.

Many investigators have attempted to solve this problem by having subjects fill out questionnaires after the bargaining procedure. Subjects might thus be asked a variety of questions about why they behaved as they did. Some investigators have even gone so far as to ask these questions after every trial. Whereas this technique is often very helpful, ultimately it is insufficient. People have a variety of ways of distorting their true goals, both to themselves and to others. In addition, the questions themselves may cause them to think about the situation in ways that would not otherwise have occurred to them. More richly variegated measures of behavior are very much needed.

2. *The utility of outcomes.* As you have undoubtedly realized, subjects typically earn very little for their efforts in bargaining. They may win points in one instance, pennies in another, or bargain for imaginary dollars in still another. Critics have often taken researchers in this area to task for making suggestions about national policy on the basis of experiments which were, to the subjects, possibly trivial in nature. To some extent this criticism is justified. And yet, the major question is whether subjects would behave any differently if the stakes were impressive and important to them. Christie, Gergen, and Marlowe (1969) attempted to shed light on this problem in an experiment in which comparisons could be made between bargaining behavior for points, pennies, or dollars. In the high-stakes condition, subjects received as many as four new, crisp one-dollar bills on each trial. They became totally enthralled as they watched the bills accumulate in front of them from trial to trial. (So impressed were they that one student at Columbia decided on the spot that he was going into psychology as a profession.) When group means were compared, however, it was found that the mean amount of exploitation was unchanged from one condition to the next. Subjects exploited in roughly equal amounts, regardless of the utilities of the outcome.

Although these data give us greater confidence in the generality of bargaining findings, they shouldn't be taken to imply that increasing the stakes never makes any difference. For one thing, in this particular study, it was found that response variability increased as one moved from pennies to dollars. That is, although the mean remained unchanged, subjects tended in the dollar condition to exploit either much more or much less than when the stakes were lower. This issue of utilities will be raised again at a later point in this chapter.

3. *Communication.* Both the present criticism and the one to follow are largely addressed to the artificiality of the bargaining relationship. The confidence one can place in generalizing from experimental studies to real-world problems is in direct proportion to the similarity of the experimental setting to the setting about which generalizations are to be made. This view, of course, holds experimental field studies at a premium. It also creates real questions about the extent to which one should generalize from most bargaining situations. One of the major ways in which most of the research on the prisoners' dilemma differs from most human interaction is that the

participants are not allowed to communicate with each other. Their impact on each other is limited to two crude behavioral alternatives, the meaning of which may be obscure for both. As we have already seen, one result of this handicap is that people often attempt to use these behaviors as forms of communication, a tendency that may often interfere with a straightforward interpretation of bargaining behavior.

The few attempts that have been made to offset this deficit are very enlightening. In the Deutsch (1960a) study of interaction goals (see p. 58), subjects in a number of conditions were also allowed to communicate freely before they finally made their decisions. The results were clear: when communication was possible prior to decision making, cooperation was maximal.

4. The range of options. Another way in which typical bargaining studies differ sharply from most social situations is that they drastically restrict the range of available options. This is not simply to say that they suffer because they have largely focused on the cooperative vs. exploitative choice to the neglect of other types of choices. Alterations in the pattern of outcomes presented in the matrix could remedy this problem. No, the more important problem is that under conditions where multiple options are available to two people, the processes of exchange may be quite different in character. Constricting the range of available options may serve to rule out of consideration many processes that are characteristic of most social relationships. For example, if we examine exploitative behavior as it typically exists, we find that in many instances exploitation is disguised or veiled by subtle maneuvers. By engaging in a host of other behaviors that are of low cost to him, the exploiter can reduce the possibility that true exploitative behavior will be perceived as such. He may thus avoid reactions of anger, reactions that are typically evoked in a bargaining situation when exploitation is recognized. Or, in daily life, a person may generate trust with a series of actions at low cost to himself, only to take advantage of the other in situations where the stakes are high; or he may actually provide the other with very positive outcomes in certain areas of exchange in order to achieve high payoffs at great cost to his partner in other areas. Such guises or trade-offs are not allowed in the basic, two-option bargaining procedure as it has been developed thus far. With a wider range of options, the high level of exploitation found in the prisoners' dilemma situation might well be dissipated.

EXPANDING HORIZONS: THREAT AND MUTUAL GAIN

Faced with the limitations of the typical bargaining approach, a number of investigators have attempted to seek alternatives. This expansion of horizons has had a salutary effect. In some cases, criticisms of the traditional bargaining research have been surmounted; in others, processes have been brought under scrutiny that had not before been capable of analysis. In terms of heuristic value, the bargaining approach has indeed been fruitful. One of the more outstanding investigations forming part of this expansion was carried out by Deutsch and Krauss (1960). It is worthwhile to discuss it in detail for several reasons. Not only is it impressive for its originality, but it begins to overcome some difficulties raised in subsections 1 and 4 in the previous section. In addition, the findings raise an intriguing argument related to the problem of negotiation and the settlement of conflict. It is not greatly surprising, then, that the research won an American Association for the Advancement of Science Award for outstanding research in the behavioral sciences.

A basic concern in this investigation was the function of threat in negotiating settlements. There are numerous instances in which two parties may be competing for conflicting ends. A union desires greater income for the workers; management wishes to reduce spending in order to keep the cost of the product at a competitive level. Socially conscious persons bring great pressure to bear on open housing, while many landowners fight for sellers' rights in order to avoid what they feel to be threat to the value of their property. And the United States seems to be in continuous turmoil in maintaining pro-Western governments in countries where there is large-scale dissatisfaction with Western ideology. But what happens to negotiation in such cases when one or both of the parties have access to threats or ways of blocking the other's actions? Unions, for example, have available the threat of strike, which can altogether block management's attempts to market goods. Social activists can now bring the federal judicial process to bear on unfair housing practices; and in the case of developing nations, war has often been used by both sides as a way of influencing settlement. Would more satisfactory solutions be reached if such means of threat were not available to the opposing sides? Does the availability of threat reduce the possibility for conciliation and achieving highest mutual gain?

To explore this problem the investigators designed a specialized bargaining procedure. Pairs of subjects (in this case, female employees of the Bell Telephone Company) were faced with a task in which each was to imagine herself in charge of a trucking company carrying merchandise over a road to a destination. For each trip completed, the subject would be paid $.60 minus her operating expenses. Operating expenses were calculated at the rate of one cent per second, and thus, it was to the subject's advantage to move to her destination as rapidly as possible. Each subject was given a name, the one Acme and the other Bolt. As the "road map" in Fig. 5.9 illustrates, each began from a separate position and had a separate destination.

The conflict of interest was created by the available routes. In order to earn the greatest amount of money, it would be most advantageous to take the shortest route (Route 216 for Acme and 106 for Bolt). However, there

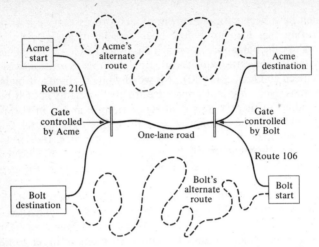

Fig. 5.9   Subjects' road map. (From Deutsch and Krauss, 1960. Copyright 1960 by the American Psychological Association, and reproduced by permission.)

was one segment of the road, common for both players, designated as "one lane." If both subjects chose the shortest route, they would run headlong into each other in the one-lane segment. In this case, either one or the other would have to back up in order that the other could go forward, or they might both continue to sit immobile and lose money.

As the figure shows, direct confrontation was not necessary. Each participant had an alternate route. This route was considerably longer (56% to be exact) than the direct route, and the amount of time needed to traverse it would cost the subject $.10 for her effort.

Given this basic conflict of interests, various conditions of threat were established by using gates. In the *Bilateral Threat* condition, both Acme and Bolt were furnished gates that would block the transit of the other. As Fig. 5.9 shows, these gates were at either end of the one-lane road. Thus, by closing her gate, Acme could prevent Bolt from reaching her destination via the shortest route, and vice versa. In the *Unilateral Threat* condition, only Acme was provided with a gate. You can well realize Acme's advantage here. If Bolt would not back down and allow Acme to proceed over the one-lane path, Acme could prevent Bolt from ever taking the route. In the *No Threat* condition, neither participant had access to a gate, and both were left to decide the use of the one-lane road as they would. Twenty trials subsequently took place, during which each participant was apprised at all times of the location of the other and of the winnings for both. Each was instructed to try to make as much money for herself as possible, but not to take an interest in how much the other was winning or losing. Unfortunately for purposes of generalization, no communication was allowed.

TABLE 5.1

Payoffs Under Varying Conditions of Threat

	No Threat	Unilateral Threat	Bilateral Threat
Acme's Payoff	122.44	−118.56	−406.56
Bolt's Payoff	80.88	−287.31	−468.56
Summed Payoff	203.31	−405.88	−875.12

Adapted from Deutsch and Krauss, 1960.

The central focus of the study was on the winnings and losses of the two players in the three conditions. The mean earnings for the various conditions can be found in Table 5.1. If we first observe the mutual gains for the participants, we quickly realize that the No Threat condition was vastly superior to either of the others. In fact, this was the only condition in which the two players actually earned any money. In the Bilateral Threat condition, the players together managed to lose almost $9.00 over the 20 trials (not actually extracted from them in the end). Under conditions of Unilateral Threat the joint losses were still high, but less than in the Bilateral Threat condition.

In breaking down these results, we find that when no threat existed both subjects won money over the 20 trials (although, for some inexplicable reason, Acme tended to earn more). Under the Unilateral Threat condition, however, Acme was able to earn an advantage by virtue of her having control of threat. To be more accurate, she managed to lose less. Never did she earn as much as she would have if neither she nor her partner had had access to threat. In the Bilateral Threat condition, both Acme and Bolt lost heavily and almost equally. It is most interesting to note here that poor Bolt's winnings under the Unilateral Threat condition were better than under Bilateral Threat. In more general terms, if one's opponent possesses the ability to threaten, in the long run one may be better off not having the capacity for counterthreat. It should also be pointed out that, in line with our earlier discussion of accommodation over time (see pp. 38-39), in both the No Threat and Unilateral Threat conditions, subjects gained increasingly higher rewards as the game proceeded. In effect, they became more and more capable of mutual accommodation.

But why should the existence of threat have been so detrimental to the participants? What mechanisms were at play? Deutsch and Krauss reasoned much as follows: if a person uses threat to intimidate another, the threatened person will under certain circumstances react with hostility, responding with either counterthreat or resistance. The person is said to gain satisfaction from having high self-esteem, and to be dissatisfied when it is taken from him. Another's use of threat reduces one's potency by comparison. To be intimidated in the form of threat is thus to undergo loss of esteem. To avoid this loss, and possibly to increase esteem through standing firm, the person reacts with counterthreat when this option is available to him. This reasoning has much in common with that of Marlowe *et al.* in studying the effects of egotism on bargaining (pp. 59-61).

Regardless of explanation, the implications of this research are very compelling. They strongly suggest that the less opportunity for threat any two parties have in negotiating a settlement, the more likely they are to share a profit in their negotiations. International settlements would be more profitable if neither party were able to threaten the other with war. Under certain conditions unions might even fare better without strikes; open housing advocates might have greater success if they did not resort to legal measures.

Whereas such an extrapolation has much to recommend it, one must still exercise a good deal of caution before making gross generalizations. For one thing, many of the conflicts to which one might want to generalize are not so easily amenable to arbitration. People's beliefs in civil rights, democracy, or communism, for example, seem to brook few compromises. In such cases people are generally unable to accept the idea of mutual gain, and they desire to see their opponents lose totally. Then too, it is quite possible that the importance or utility of the outcomes (see p. 65) may place limitations on these data. In following up the initial work by Deutsch and Krauss, Gallo (1966) found that by increasing the amount of money that subjects could gain through cooperation, even bilateral threat could be made into a winning proposition.

If there is one general conclusion that might be reached after this lengthy discussion of interpersonal bargaining, it is that for any exchange between two people there may be multiple sources of satisfaction, and intricate processes may be involved in bringing about maximization. The ways in which persons go about gaining these rewards in a complex world have, of course, been the central thread running through the research we have discussed. It must be concluded, however, that even though we know a good deal about peoples' overt behavior in such situations, our understanding of the underlying processes is much more slim.

REFERENCES

Adorno, T. W., Else Frenkel-Brunswik, D. J. Levinson, and R. N. Sanford, *The Authoritarian Personality*. New York: Harper, 1950.

Braithwaite, R. B., *Theory of Games as a Tool for the Moral Philosophy*. Cambridge: Cambridge University Press, 1955.

Brehm, J. W., *A Theory of Psychological Reactance*. New York: Academic Press, 1966.

Christie, R., K. J. Gergen, and D. Marlowe, The penny-dollar caper, in *Studies in Machiavellianism* (R. Christie and F. Geis, eds.). New York: Academic Press, 1969.

Deutsch, M., The effect of motivational orientation upon trust and suspicion. *Human Relations,* **13,** 123-139, 1960a.

Deutsch, M., Trust, trustworthiness, and the *F* scale. *Journal of Abnormal and Social Psychology,* **61,** 138-140, 1960b.

Deutsch, M., and R. M. Krauss, The effect of threat upon interpersonal bargaining. *Journal of Abnormal and Social Psychology,* **61,** 168-175, 1960.

Gallo, P. S., Effects of increased incentives upon the use of threat in bargaining. *Journal of Personality and Social Psychology,* **4,** 14-20, 1966.

Gergen, K. J., and B. Wishnov, Other's self-evaluations and interaction anticipation as determinants of self-presentation. *Journal of Personality and Social Psychology,* **3,** 348-358, 1965.

Luce, R. D., and H. Raiffa, *Games and Decisions.* New York: John Wiley and Sons, 1957.

Marlowe, D., K. J. Gergen, and A. N. Doob, Opponent's personality, expectation of social interaction, and interpersonal bargaining. *Journal of Personality and Social Psychology,* **3,** 206-213, 1966.

Minas, J. S., A. Scodel, D. Marlowe, and H. Rawson, Some descriptive aspects of two-person non-zero-sum games. *Journal of Conflict Resolution,* **4,** 193-197, 1960.

Rapoport, A., *Fights, Games and Debates.* Ann Arbor: University of Michigan Press, 1960.

Rapoport, A., *Two-Person Game Theory.* Ann Arbor: University of Michigan Press, 1966.

Rapoport, A., and A. M. Chammah, *Prisoners' Dilemma: A Study of Conflict and Cooperation.* Ann Arbor: University of Michigan Press, 1965.

Thibaut, J. W., and H. H. Kelley, *The Social Psychology of Groups.* New York: John Wiley and Sons, 1959.

Von Neumann, J., and O. Morgenstern, *Theory of Games and Economic Behavior.* Princeton: Princeton University Press, 1944.

Williams, J. D., *The Compleat Strategyst.* New York: McGraw-Hill, 1954.

CHAPTER SIX

Patterned Interaction:
Norms and Roles

One problem with many psychological experiments is that they take place in such a short span of time that one fails to see phenomena born of long-term relationships. In most research, considerations of rigor and validity require that subjects not have detailed information about the person with whom they are to interact—information that might bias their behavior in such a way that the effects of the experimental variables are obscured or confounded. Thus, the special aspects of relationships, aspects that only develop with time, have often escaped attention. Fortunately, not all such phenomena have been so neglected. In particular, the one phenomenon of this ilk that has long aroused the curiosity of social psychologists is the seeming tendency for social relationships to move toward stability, a tendency that appears to have a strange power over the recipients. This statement may sound almost mystical, connoting some form of spiritual inertia or gravity. Let us put the case less abstractly and see if it becomes more palatable from a scientific standpoint.

If we observe the behavior of any two persons over time, we find that certain patterns develop with overwhelming frequency. Day after day, and often over a span of years, the two individuals will react more and more predictably to each other. Particular patterns of exchange will be followed almost to the letter. This is not to say there are never deviations. But most instances of turbulence or marked fluctuation within the dyad can be traced to changes that have occurred in the environment. Individuals change *in reaction to* novel occurrences impinging on the relationship (e.g., a newborn baby, a new job, a death in the family). The patterns are seldom broken as a result of factors intrinsic to the relationship itself. That the pattern comes to have power over the individuals is a part of the argument that we must put aside until we have asked ourselves *why* the tendency toward patterned interaction exists.

These relatively stable and enduring patterns of behavior within a relationship we shall call *norms*. In a statistical sense, they represent central tendencies around which there may be minor variations—in this case, behavioral tendencies of the participants. But why should norms develop? What is behind the "force" toward stabilization? And be careful to note that this question is not merely academic. When you stop to think that the very relationships that you esteem so highly because of their spontaneous, impulsive quality are possibly doomed because of this force, the problem takes on much personal significance.

A number of factors produce this stability in interpersonal relationships:

1. Maximizing satisfaction. As you will recall from our initial diagram of the exchange matrix, various combinations of behavior yield varying amounts of satisfaction or dissatisfaction to the participants. If each searches for maximum satisfaction or payoffs in the relationship, and there is ample latitude for shifting one's behavior and sampling various combinations, a set of maximal value combinations should eventually be found. This process is the essence of accommodation. Once this arrangement is discovered, there is little reason to discontinue it. When a particular set of combinations yields maximum satisfaction (at least for that relationship), why should one slip into behavior sequences that yield inferior payoffs? Over the years, an elderly couple may have found that a particular pattern of daily living maintains them both at a high level of satisfaction. In various formal exchanges, such as those of the marketplace, the exchange of money for goods has become sufficiently satisfying that almost the entire society participates in the norm. (Most of the others are in prison.)

2. The value of predictability. A good deal of recent research indicates that a disordered, nonlogical, or unpredictable world is dissatisfying to people. Inconsistency, at least in gross amounts, is aversive, and the person strives to avoid such conditions. The literature on cognitive dissonance (cf. Festinger, 1957; Brehm and Cohen, 1962; Zimbardo and Ebbesen, 1969) is impressive because it demonstrates the extreme and irrational lengths to which people will go in order to reestablish order and consistency.

While there is little reason to suppose that the dissatisfaction produced by inconsistency is genetically based, it does seem quite possible that persons could learn to avoid such conditions. After all, it is the ordered and consistent world that best allows the person to maximize his returns. If he can be sure that each time he behaves in one way he will be rewarded, and that for other actions he will be punished, he will be in a position to maximize his satisfaction. If the environment is capricious, his capacity to make a "correct" choice is destroyed. In effect, the state of consistency has a *learned* payoff value, and the individual is trained to devalue the state of disorder.

This need for consistency is quite relevant to the stabilization of norms in a relationship. Norms instill order into a relationship. Normative behavior is behavior that one can depend on; it allows one to operate successfully within the relationship. From this viewpoint it is easy to see why members of various minority groups, fringe elements, extremists, and the mentally ill fall prey to so much prejudice. Their behavior seems unpredictable and thus unsafe. Greater familiarity should thus yield greater acceptance.

3. Restraint of power. Thibaut and Kelley (1959) have pointed out that the unrestrained use of power by one person over another creates difficulties for both. If the stronger fully exercises his power, he may be forced into the undesirable activity of monitoring the behavior of the less powerful. The less powerful, on the other hand, is likely to experience poorer outcomes (less satisfaction) should power be used to dictate all his actions. Norms thus become a way of insulating both members of the relationship from the unbridled use of power.

4. Secondary gain. If, for all these various reasons, norms have utility in a relationship, then having norms in itself may develop its own independent value. According to elementary principles of conditioning, a stimulus may come to have reward value simply because it is associated with another stimulus that provides a basic satisfaction. If one has always received loving nurturance in the home in which he grew up, merely visiting the home without the parents' presence may later be strangely satisfying. Many "friends" probably remain in that status primarily because of the positive experiences they had together long before—experiences they may be totally unable to repeat. In the same way, norms themselves may provide this secondary gain, even if the rewards discussed above are not available. Leaderless training groups—an increasingly popular activity designed to improve skills in communication and understanding—often illustrate this phenomenon. Such groups typically have no leader and no standard schedule or specified aims or activities—in effect, no norms. The anguish that most people feel as a result is often unbearable, and many will quickly set about to create norms, even when such norms have no clear function.

Now that we have seen why norms develop, we can turn to the second part of our mystical premise: that the tendency toward stability comes to have power over the participants in a relationship. What does it mean to say that norms have power over people? The intent here is to point to the widespread tendency for normative behavior to become formalized and buttressed by positive and negative sanctions. This is to say that what is typical or usual comes to have a certain sanctity. The usual becomes ritual, and ritual becomes regulation. Goffman (1963) has argued that people who do not behave as the norms prescribe are placed in mental institutions. The society cannot tolerate those who refuse to abide by the rituals of everyday life. In many cases, this formalization may even reach the point of being spelled out in a series of laws. Special policing functions may be established, and violators punished or even extinguished. The laws of the land can be viewed as a formalization of the normative ways people have generally found to maximize joint payoff.

It remains an open question why the transition from informal mores to forced compliance takes place, either within the dyad or in society. Possibly, the process is activated when the informal arrangement, so highly satisfactory to the participants, is threatened by some outside force. If the people of a society find the typical marriage arrangement generally beneficial, they might be more apt to outlaw prostitution, a threat to marital sanctity. A government that found itself truly threatened by public demonstration might create formal laws curtailing civil liberties.

It also seems that the greater the satisfaction group members receive for a certain activity, the more likely they are to guarantee its continued existence through formalization. Business organizations find that their very existence depends on a given set of exchanges among their employees, and thus establish company regulations. And athletic teams whose sole aim is to win set up training regulations and punish those who violate them. Just what conditions foster this transition from informal patterns to formal laws has never been studied systematically, but is much deserving of attention.

Of course, norms need not reach the stage of formal rules before they are used to shape conduct. In fact, one of the most interesting areas of inquiry for social psychologists has been the process by which groups bring conformity pressure to bear on their members. The Kieslers' contribution to the present series (Kiesler and Kiesler, 1969) concentrates on such processes in detail.

The various principles dealing with norm enforcement and conformity are usually considered relevant to any norm, that is, to be highly general. Indeed they may be, but to close off discussion of norms at this point would cause us to miss out on one of the most central lines of research within the social exchange framework. From the standpoint of exchange, not only the general processes relevant to norms are important, but also the operation of specific types of norms. For example, there are certain norms relevant to relationships between high- and low-power persons as opposed to groups of equals, and so on. Because of its pervasive and possibly global influence, one particular type of norm has been most closely studied in the exchange framework. This is the norm of social reciprocity.

RECIPROCITY IN INTERPERSONAL RELATIONS

The principle of reciprocity has made its way into the literature in many different forms (cf. Simmel, 1950; Homans, 1958; and Gouldner, 1960). The one central proposition that can be drawn from the work in this area is that there is a strong tendency on the part of individuals to respond in kind to the behavior they receive. If rewards or satisfactions are received from another, there is a tendency to provide rewards in return; if dissatisfaction is received, the response is to punish the other. Some have viewed this tendency as a basic cornerstone in social ethics. Its formal expression is represented in the "eye for an eye, tooth for a tooth" concept of justice, or in the intonement to "do unto others as you would have them do unto you." In his analysis of morality in society, the early ethicist, Edvard Westermarck, pointed out in 1908 that "To requite a benefit or to be grateful to him who bestows it, is probably everywhere, at least under certain conditions, regarded as a duty." Sociologists have even seen this tendency as basic to the survival of a stable society.

But what lies behind the development of such a norm? If there is such a pervasive tendency, what need does it fill in society? This is a difficult question indeed, because the norm now seems handed on, from one generation to the next, without question. Children learn the norm at a very early age. They learn to be "fair," and to do favors in return, just as they learn that they have a "right" to hit back if struck. But precisely how the norm originated, and what value it has at present, remains unclear.

Any final solution to this question will certainly have to distinguish between benefit and harm. Different processes may underly the "eye for an eye" mentality as contrasted with the necessity for returning kindness with good. Punishing someone who does harm may serve to prevent people from exploiting each other. When the penal code operates on an eye-for-an-eye basis, the man in the street may feel more secure. He may feel that others will be fearful of committing crime. Unprovoked harm may also create frustration, blocking people from anticipated goals, depriving them of rewards. And if the tendency for aggression to follow frustration is instinctive, as much animal work would suggest, the reciprocity norm would furnish a publicly sanctioned channel for expressing aggression. The death penalty in the United States is obviously relevant to this issue. It may be less a deterrent to crime than a way for people to express their aggressions in a publicly acceptable way.

But what about reciprocity of the more benign variety? Why is it that people tend to return positive outcomes in kind. This tendency may in part grow out of people's basic dislike of providing rewards to another at a cost to self. To ensure a return on such costs, people may have made it a duty for the recipient to return the benefit. National governments are loath, for example, to provide foreign aid solely for humanitarian purposes. Instead, all governments require some type of return on their investments. What appears as aid is in reality an exchange. But the norm of benign reciprocity may also be a way of insulating individuals (or oneself) against exploitation. Thus society tries to prevent one man's rewards from becoming another's losses. People are obliged to reciprocate for what they take. Our legal codes fully support this value. Possibly, the ability to experience vicarious dissatisfaction may also be at stake. The dissatisfaction felt through vicariously experiencing another's loss, which has become your gain, can be reduced by providing gain in return. Others have poked fun at Americans for years because the same countries we destroy in war, we devote long years of labor to rebuilding. The Israelis have even joked that the best way of improving their economy would be to declare war on the United States.

RECIPROCITY AND FOREIGN AID

Although we lack sufficient data to answer this question of origin, we can ask about the extent to which the reciprocity norm exists, and whether its effects can be demonstrated. One study relevant to the norm and suggesting its pervasiveness across cultural boundaries was carried out by Gergen, Diebold, Seipel, and Gresser (in preparation). This experiment was conducted in the United States, Sweden, and Japan and used college-age males as subjects. The primary concern of the study was the effects of gifts or favors on attitudes of the receiver toward the giver. The real-world problem stimulating this line of research was how a country could best go about building goodwill abroad through giving foreign aid. The United States, for example, typically budgets between two and four billion dollars a year for foreign aid. It is often assumed that this aid will secure the friendship of the recipient peoples. In point of fact, there are a number of instances in which just the opposite seems to have occurred. Rather than positive regard, aid seems to have produced resentment or hostility. The problem, then, is to determine the set of conditions under which a positive response is most likely.

As was pointed out earlier, social exchange is closely related to social attraction. We simply need to add the supposition that positive payoffs or satisfactions yield attraction, while dissatisfaction creates hostility toward the agent responsible for the state. In the case of reciprocity, it would follow from what was said above that, when another provides a reciprocal exchange, he should be more appreciated or liked than if he proposes less than a reciprocal arrangement. If reciprocity is the preferred state, then another who is responsible for a nonreciprocal arrangement should be less well liked.

When we apply this thinking to the problem of foreign aid, the question becomes, "How much obligation should be attached to the resources supplied to another country?" A completely reciprocal arrangement would be one in which the recipient is asked to return the aid he receives. Two nonreciprocal arrangements are possible. In the first, more would be asked in return than is given (e.g., a high rate of interest on a loan). When compared with the reciprocal arrangement, it is very clear which would be the inferior from the recipient's viewpoint. Unfortunately, however, one need not invoke the reciprocity principle to make the prediction that reciprocity would be preferred in this case. When a high rate of interest is being charged or many favors asked in return, the recipient is simply receiving less in the way of absolute satisfaction. The satisfaction produced by the gift has to be reduced by its cost to him, and returning the favor *plus* interest is more expensive than merely returning the favor. There is more than one reason, then, to dislike a gift with high obligation attached.

The more interesting and crucial test of the hypothesis that reciprocity is desirable comes when we compare the reciprocal arrangement with one in which the gift is given without *any* obligation attached. Here again the situation is nonreciprocal; the recipient is receiving without being asked for anything in return. However, he is also receiving more benefit on an absolute scale than in the reciprocal condition. If the reciprocal arrangement is still preferred, in spite of the inferior level of rewards otherwise being received, then we would indeed have to conclude that reciprocity is a strong source of satisfaction.

To explore the effects of the various conditions of reciprocity, an experiment was developed in which subjects worked at a competitive task to obtain money. Six subjects participated at a time, and each was placed in a separate experimental booth. The session was said to take place in two parts. In the first all subjects would be required to wager their resources on various chance outcomes. In effect, they were to gamble with some $3.00 worth of chips which had been supplied to them. In the second part of the experiment they were to pair off with each other, and the pairs were to play against each other for additional resources. The chips could be cashed in for money at the end of the competition.

The game of chance was so arranged that all subjects lost heavily in the betting procedure. However, while each was losing, the experimenter made public announcements of winnings and losses of the players. These announcements made it appear to each subject that his losses were greatest, and that other players were prospering in varying degrees. Late in the betting procedure each subject was confronted with a wager that, should he lose, would deplete his supply of chips entirely. He might then be forced out of the competition altogether. Just at that moment, in the nick of time, each player received an envelope containing a gift of 10 chips. The gift appeared to have come from one of the other participants.

The gift of chips had a note attached. The note had been specially prepared in one of three ways. A third of the subjects, chosen at random, were given the gift of 10 chips under the first of the nonreciprocal arrangements discussed above; they were asked for more in return than they received. The note asked that the chips be returned with interest at the end of the session and that the subject plan to do the giver a favor later on (High Obligation condition). A second group of subjects was confronted with a nonreciprocal arrangement of the second variety, one in which nothing was asked in return. The note said that the subject could keep the money and need not bother returning it (Low Obligation condition). The third group of subjects received the chips under a reciprocal condition. The note simply

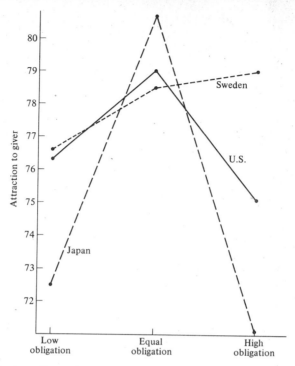

Fig. 6.1 Reciprocity and attraction to a gift giver. (Adapted from Gergen, Diebold, Seipel, and Gresser, in preparation.)

asked that the chips be returned at the end of the session (Equal Obligation condition). Parenthetically, the gift did prove to be useful to the subjects before the gambling procedure had been completed.

Although the study was also concerned with other factors, we shall confine ourselves to the effects of obligation on the feelings of attraction the recipients had for the givers. The subjects were thus asked, after the gambling had been completed, to make a series of ratings of any participant who might have sent them a note. Since all other notes written by the subjects had been intercepted, and all subjects had received the one specially devised note, the ratings were of the fictitious but psychologically real benefactor. Imbedded in the ratings was a set of scales that were evaluatively loaded (e.g., friendly-unfriendly, likable-not likable). The primary question was whether the differing amounts of obligation would affect these attraction ratings.

The ratings were collapsed into a single attraction measure. The mean attraction toward the giver in each of the three conditions for each of the countries is displayed in Fig. 6.1. As can be seen, there is a dramatic tendency for the gift giver who provides a reciprocal exchange arrangement to be preferred. In both Japan and the United States, the effects are marked. Only with Swedish subjects is there an irregularity in the pattern. In this case the equal-obligation giver is liked more than the low-obligation giver, as was predicted. The unexpected finding is that the high-obligation giver is liked most (although the result is not statistically reliable). Possibly in Sweden the concept of usury has different connotations than in the other two countries, and a stronger manipulation of high obligation is necessary to bring out the curvilinear relationship. However, the most important fact is that, of the six comparisons relevant to the prediction that reciprocity is preferred, five are strongly supportive.

Additional data are needed. Why the attraction to the low-obligation giver is so very low, especially in comparison to the high-obligation giver, is not clear. It may be that in industrialized societies such as the United States, Japan, or Sweden, charging interest is not viewed as particularly inequitable but as having some justification. Returning to the issue of foreign aid, however, the research suggests that obligation-free gifts are likely to be less effective than no-interest loans in building goodwill. Apparently people do not really appreciate something for nothing. In addition, the giving country loses fewer resources under conditions of reciprocity.

RECIPROCITY AND BEHAVIOR IN THE BUSINESS WORLD

We can now turn from the relationship of reciprocity to attitudes, to ask about behavior. Is it possible to demonstrate, for example, that if a person is faced with a nonreciprocal arrangement, he will try to alter the situation so as to produce reciprocity? Some of the most interesting data on this problem come from research in business and industrial settings. As you can well imagine, the issues of what constitutes a "just" wage and what workers will do when they feel they are not receiving just returns are of great importance in our economy. Unless there is widespread agreement between management and workers as to what is *equitable*, the entire economic structure could collapse.

For our purposes, "justice" and "equity" are forms of the reciprocity norm at play. People generally believe their contribution to the business organization should be matched by an equal return. The relationship between what they contribute and what is contributed to them should be reciprocal. Adams (1965) has dealt with this problem in terms of the ratio of *inputs* to *outcomes*. From his viewpoint, workers desire equity between their inputs (in terms of their contribution to the business) and their outcomes (their salary). There is both an obvious and a nonobvious implication of this formulation. The more obvious one is that when workers feel their pay is *less* than their contribution, they will take steps to alter either their salary or their inputs (services rendered). The strike is the most dramatic way in which pressure is applied to increase salary. There is less evidence, possibly because it is more difficult to obtain, on the way in which workers will modify inputs or work effort to reduce inequity.

One of the most engaging examples of reducing inputs is provided by Clark (1958) in a study of supermarket operations. A substantial portion of the cost of operating a supermarket is accounted for by the salaries of cashiers and their working partners, the package handlers. If these pairs work with speed and efficiency (and no one who has ever waited in a long checkout line will agree they do), the cost of operating the supermarket is that much lower. Now, as Adams (1965) has shown, whether a person feels his salary to be equitable or not is largely dependent on what he observes around him. This is to say that not only is the concept of reciprocity a social norm, but so is the conception of *what* is reciprocal. At any rate, Clark found that both cashiers and package handlers largely judged the equity of their salary by comparing themselves with each other. For example, if a college-educated male of 21 found that he, as a package handler, was making less money than the cashier, a 17-year-old high school girl, he would tend to feel that his relationship with the management was not a reciprocal one. From his point of view, his skills and age allowed him to contribute more to the business than his pay merited.

Interviews with package handlers revealed that the primary way in which they reduced inequity was by decreasing the rate at which they filled bags. In essence, they reduced their input in effort. When eight separate supermarkets were ranked on labor efficiency (number of man-hours required per $100 sales) and on "social ease" (an index of the amount of inequity existing within the cashier-handler pairs), it was found that the two measures correlated almost perfectly. In effect, the greater the social inequity, the greater the cost of operating the store. In that store where greatest inequity existed (and presumably reciprocity was least), operating costs were 27% higher than in the store in which equitable working relationships were maintained.

Benign Inequity

That workers will strike or reduce their efficiency because they feel they are not receiving just compensation is an important fact, but not altogether surprising. The more intriguing implication of the equity formulation is that if workers find their outputs or salaries are *greater* than their inputs or efforts, they should also react negatively. Instead of merely wanting as high a salary as possible, they will want a salary that is equivalent to their contribution. This derivation is parallel to the foreign aid study discussed above. As you will recall, the subjects were not attracted to the giver who provided something for nothing.

When that which is received from another exceeds that which is given to him in return, the condition is one of *benign inequity*. This condition may be contrasted with the *malignant* variety in which one's contribution exceeds his compensation. A person's behavioral reaction to benign inequity may be one of two kinds. He can either increase his inputs to the organization, or attempt to decrease the rewards he is receiving. There is very little evidence in support of the latter of these alternatives. People don't seem to want to give up salary when they find their work is not demanding enough. Rather, in order to reestablish reciprocity, people seem much more inclined to increase their costs or inputs. A study by Adams and Jacobson (1964) is most enlightening here.

These investigators hired students as proofreaders for manuscript copy. At random, each student was placed in one of three conditions. In the High Inequity condition, subjects were told that they were unqualified for the job, but nevertheless they would be paid the same amount as standard proofreaders ($.30 a page). Subjects in the remaining two conditions (Reduced Inequity) were exposed to a salary arrangement that was more reciprocal. In one of these conditions they were told that because of their lack of qualifications their pay would be only $.20 instead of the normal pay rate for qualified personnel. In effect, the outputs were commensurate with the inputs that could be expected from the students. In the final condition the students were told that they were fully qualified to earn the $.30 a page, and would thus be paid at this rate.

The major focus of the study was on the effects of these variations in equity on the quality of the work done by the students. If reciprocity is a valued state, then it would be predicted that the highest-quality work should be turned in by those in the High Inequity condition. These subjects alone were faced with rewards that exceeded their costs, and thus should work more diligently to compensate. In order to measure work quality, the average number of errors detected on the page proofs was assessed for each of the three conditions. It had been arranged that all subjects proofread the same material, and the number of errors imbedded in the material was constant. The results fully supported the hypothesis. The average number of errors detected per page was higher for the High Inequity condition than for either of the others, and the difference was statistically significant. In fact, subjects in this condition were so intent on their work that they were even more likely to challenge words that were in fact correct. These results have interesting implications for management. They suggest that rewards provided *before* performance may have just as strong effects as those given after, possibly increasing morale at the same time. Giving a raise before it is felt to be "deserved" may increase dedication to the job.

SOCIAL ROLES AS INDIVIDUALIZED NORMS

Much has been said concerning the function of norms within social relationships and the ways in which certain norms may influence behavior. At the same time, we have glossed over the fact that norms may be individualized. We have spoken of norms as if they were totally democratic, affecting everyone equally. And yet it is very clear in most groups, from two persons to a society, that this is untrue. As we look about us we quickly see that while there are some norms that affect almost all people, others are specific to certain subgroups or even to specific individuals. While the bulk of the population may be subject to the norms embodied in the legal structure, there are other norms for doctors which differ from those followed by policemen. Or within small groups there may be norms common to all members, but certain patterns of behavior followed only by the leader. In marriage both partners may follow some norms, but the husband's behavior pattern is expected to differ from his wife's. It is these more differentiated behavioral norms that are captured in the concept of *social role.*

In some ways, the concept of social role may be unparsimonious—an unnecessary term in the theory. All the principles governing norm development and formalization, communication, and conformity should apply to the norms governing the behavior of single individuals. From this viewpoint, we need only think in terms of the class of persons to whom the norm is relevant; the principles of norm behavior should remain the same. However, there are some social scientists who would strenuously object to doing away with the additional concept of role on the grounds that the concept implies more than behavioral patterning. Rather, they would say, the major feature of roles is their *functional* value. Roles are not simply patterns of behavior, but they play a crucial part in maintaining the existence of a group. In order to maintain itself, the society requires differentiation into various roles, so that various subgroups each make a specific contribution to the whole. For instance, almost all cultures require a "healer," whether he be a doctor or a medicine man. On the other hand, there is nothing in this latter approach that disagrees with what we have said thus far. Norm behavior is generally that which provides maximal payoffs for the majority of the participants. In essence, norm behavior is typically functional in this broader sense.

A voluminous amount of literature on role behavior exists for the reader who wishes to examine the area more carefully. Much of it documents the norms within various subgroups of society, and the contribution these patterns make to the polity. Other investigators have studied the unfortunate person whose formal role brings him face to face with different groups which expect different things from him. This is the area of role conflict. Still other researchers have delved into the problems people have in moving from one role or normative pattern to another. Such literature suggests that, even though the concept of role is superfluous on a theoretical level, it may serve as a useful orienting term for the study of certain problems. And since these problems are not all the same—as we move from one social or occupational group to another—it becomes useful to speak of different *types* of roles. The study of the leadership role is a good case in point.

LEADERSHIP ROLES IN GROUPS

For years social psychologists have attempted to fathom that curious process by which a single individual in a group comes to have influence over the behavior of the others. Of course, for many groups there are highly articulated norms that specify who shall lead and how. The military organization is only one example. But even in the unstructured training group to which we alluded earlier, we continuously observe leadership patterns emerging without benefit of formalized norms. Somehow, one member comes to have a much greater impact on the course of events in the group than would be his if complete democracy prevailed. Both the early Romans and later the Florentines gave up democratic forms of society in favor of autocracy. What is behind such phenomena? Why do groups of people seem to move so easily from a state of equality to one in which lines of authority prevail?

Over the years, two lines of thinking on this problem have held sway. On the one hand, researchers have been impressed with the particular personalities of people who occupy dominant positions. Such research, for example, has measured people on a variety of dimensions and then examined which measures best predict who becomes a leader in a group. In the literature on small groups, we find that group members have been measured on such dimensions as intelligence, social sensitivity, empathy, need for social approval, dominance needs, and so on. The assumptions underlying such research are twofold: first, that certain individuals, by virtue of their particular styles of interpersonal behavior, are sought out by others for leadership positions; and second, that certain individuals, by virtue of their particular needs or motivations, most wish to lead.

As reasonable as these ideas appear, the research results have been mediocre at best. To be sure, persons high on a particular trait are found to be leaders in one setting; but soon another researcher will discover the opposite relationship in another setting, and a third, no relationship at all. For example, in Mann's (1959) extensive review of the literature in this area, 13 different studies were found in which intelligence was correlated with leadership. In seven, the more intelligent were more popular, five showed no relationship, and one showed the more intelligent to be less preferred. Of 78 tests of the relationship between adjustment and leadership, only 15 yielded a significant positive relationship, while 19 suggested that the most adjusted were less preferred.

From this first viewpoint it is the "great and singularly motivated men" who make history. A second major line of investigation, however, has disregarded personal characteristics and looked, rather, on the structure of the situation. From this second stance, the so-called "great men" are viewed more as accidents. They just happened to be at the right place at the right time, and the forces of historical process carried them along. Biographers have long wrestled with this problem by searching out the details of a man's life and his times. Social psychologists, on the other hand, have attempted to demonstrate this premise of "situational determination" by experimentation. Situations can be structured in various ways, and by placing individuals at random within the structure, leadership or influence can be predicted on the basis of where in the structure the person is placed. You may already be acquainted with the classic work of Leavitt (1951), in which various communication networks were arranged for task-oriented groups. It was found that persons occupying central positions in the communication network invariably came to be seen as leaders by the remainder of the group.

While the situational approach does make a good deal of sense, its applicability is clearly limited. Small, informal groups are not structured along such formal lines, and still, leaders emerge in such groups. In addition, when various persons have occupied the same formal position, such as the presidency, it is quickly realized that some are more effective leaders than others (although any leader's "effectiveness" depends on who is writing the history at the time). Clearly we need to go further than the situational approach alone can take us. As you may have guessed from this digression into the history of leadership research, the exchange approach does go the extra step.

Viewing leadership from the exchange framework, we are sensitized to two questions: (1) who in a group is most capable of maximizing satisfaction and minimizing dissatisfaction for others (the "majority" in the case of a democratic group structure), and (2) for whom would a position of high influence offer the greatest personal rewards. In the first case, we are asking about the individual's capability to provide payoffs to others; and in the second, about personal needs that might cause a person to engage in the behavior necessary to become leader. Lest this begin to sound like a simple reformulation of the individual-differences approach to leadership, one very important clause needs to be added: satisfaction for group members depends on the particular situation in which the group exists.

Let us elaborate on the last statement. Behavior which is rewarding to group members will depend on their need state at the given time. This need state will be vitally affected by the context in which the group functions. A group that is lost in the desert will most likely place its reliance on that man most able to lead them to water; a group suffering from boredom, on that man who is most able to provide novelty. In the case of the Romans and Florentines, it has been ventured that because of their state of affluence (or lack of overwhelming need) and the burdens of responsibility that democratic institutions imposed, they were only too happy to turn to autocracy.* As a corollary to this last proposition, the motives that may be

---

*Professor John Benson of St. Peter's College may be consulted for his extensive research on the underlying dynamics of the Roman case.

satisfied by leadership may also change with the situation. In some cases the major reward in leadership is group adoration. Thus, the man who is satiated with social approval may be little motivated to lead. Likewise, if the major reward were monetary, few millionaires would go to the effort of striving for leadership. Both the Caesars in early Rome and the Medicis in later Florence also appeared to have personal needs that positions of public authority satisfied at the time.

While little is known about the situational dependence of the leaders' needs, Homans (1961) has provided an excellent example of the relativity of group needs. Homans carried out a sensitive reanalysis of data collected by Helen Jennings in a classic study of leadership in a state training school for juvenile sex offenders. Among other things, each girl indicated the names of other inmates with whom she would most like to live and work. A sociometric analysis was then used to identify the most and least popular girls in the training school. Also available were a variety of ratings of the girls by their housemothers. Homans called special attention to those characteristics most often ascribed to the most popular (over-chosen) girls. Specifically they were characterized by the housemothers as "even in disposition," "willing to do more than their share of the work," "able to plan," and so on. Such characteristics might cause the girls to be popular with both the other girls and the housemothers alike. At the same time, however, these same girls were most often seen by the housemothers as "rebellious," "retaliatory," and "reticent." These were clearly not characteristics that the housemothers would appreciate or feel were desirable. Such girls would hardly be most popular among the housemothers. But for the inmates these same behaviors were apt to be prized. In rebelling, in retaliating, or in being reticent, these over-chosen girls were carrying out actions that the remainder of the inmates most likely admired and which gratified their particular needs. While Homans' analysis makes excellent use of findings from a field setting, Hollander's work on idiosyncrasy credit (to be discussed in the following section) comes to grips with the problem more scientifically, and at the same time allows us to add in an important way to our theory.

THE CREDIT TO DEVIATE

We have said that the person who provides greatest satisfaction to the group in its particular situation gains value for the members and becomes the group leader. As leader, his behavior will become hedged by norms. Persons will come to rely on him for benefit, and the arrangement will rapidly become normative and then buttressed by sanctions. This process has led many investigators to conclude that the leader of a group may have less freedom of action than any other member. The punishment that would result should he deviate from the norms relevant to his position would be greater than for any other group member.

As logical as this conclusion seems, the data on leadership and conformity are far from supportive. In fact, a number of studies show that those who are most in control take *more* liberties, have greater freedom. How can these results be reconciled with the previous reasoning? Do generals have more or less freedom than enlisted personnel, executives more or less than blue collar workers, student leaders more or less than their followers?

Hollander (1958, 1964) proposes a solution to the problem that both fits and expands the exchange model in an interesting way. He proposes that the benefit provided by a leader to a group over time is much like money placed in a bank. Benefits accumulate and establish a fund of credit, termed *idiosyncrasy credit* by Hollander. In essence, once the leader has accumulated a certain amount of idiosyncrasy credit, he may deviate from the norm without fear of recrimination. At the same time, his deviancy acts to reduce credit. With credit reduction comes loss in power to influence. The leader is at once bound and free. He is bound in the sense that others depend on him for outcomes, but the benefits he provides them over time establish his freedom—a freedom that wanes with use.

Experimental support does exist for these suppositions. In one study, carried out by Hollander in 1960, a number of five-man groups were put to work on an exceedingly difficult (actually insoluble) task. The task required that a number of group decisions be reached, and, depending on the correctness of these decisions, the group would receive monetary rewards. None of the group members knew each other prior to the task, so that complete equality in influence existed at the outset. By experimental arrangement, there were essentially two types of rewards that a group member could provide for the others. First, he could suggest solutions that would enable them all to receive a high monetary payoff. Second, he could obey the rules for making decisions, rules that the group had established before the decision trials began (i.e., in what order members should speak, majority rule, etc.). Theoretically, the person providing these various rewards in greatest abundance should come to be leader, and in this case, have the greatest amount of influence over group decisions.

In this study an experimental confederate continuously provided the first type of the above-mentioned rewards to the group. By design, his suggestion for group choice was almost always more nearly correct than any others. The theory would predict, then, that he should have greatest influence over the decisions of the group, and over time this influence should increase. However, in the second of the reward domains, "the hero's" behavior was not always so satisfying to his colleagues. He spoke out of turn, objected to majority rule, and was otherwise cantankerous. Various experimental groups were exposed to varying amounts of deviancy on his part, and at various periods in the 15-trial procedure. Theoretically, such behavior should expend his credit, and cause him to lose his capacity to influence.

The results of the study first showed that providing rewards to the group in the form of correct judgments caused the confederate to develop influence capacity. The others followed his judgments more and more as the trials progressed. While far from surprising, these results do demonstrate the cumulative impact of providing satisfaction to group members. More interesting were the effects of deviation. Here it was found that deviation from the norms caused the confederate to lose influence over the group. After those occasions on which he was unruly, the group was less likely to agree with his suggested solutions. Deviations from the norm, then, appear to act as debits, and drain one's capacity to influence the group by his judgments— even though these judgments are quite accurate.

We should not leave the concept of *idiosyncrasy credit* without adding one final note relevant to our theory. In the research on bargaining, we saw that the immediate rewards available in a situation affect behavior in a profound way. People change their behavior as the rewards in the situation are altered. The concept of *idiosyncrasy credit* extends our perspective in a very important way. It suggests that in predicting behavior at a given moment, we must take account not only of the immediately available rewards, but of the total amount of reward and punishment received in the relationship to date. Rewards received from another person in the remote past are stored, and may influence our behavior toward him in the present. The reciprocity norm may also operate in this fashion. Like the elephant, people don't seem to forget favors or punishments from the past and may reciprocate at any moment. This is no small matter, either conceptually or interpersonally. The matter of interpersonal trust, or faith in the constancy of the other, depends in large measure on just this ability to store rewards like credit in a bank. Without such a capacity, a person's behavior might be totally chameleon-like, changing with the contingencies of the moment. When we have established credit, we can expect another to remain steadfast in spite of our current failings.

THE PERSONAL COST OF NORMS

Thus far we have not attempted to draw any conclusions as to the relative "goodness" of norms in human relationships. After all, there is nothing that specifically qualifies a behavioral scientist to make evaluative judgments any more than the next man. On the other hand, because there is a strong tendency for people to sanctify "that which is," it is important before moving on to note the often hidden costs of social norms. We have spoken of norms in terms of the participants maximizing their satisfaction. However, it is important to be aware that this does not imply that persons receive the maximal amount of satisfaction of which they are capable. On the contrary, it is rather to say that people make the most of what is available, however poor their return may be. The principle of maximization, then, could lead a person simply to reduce as much as possible the amount of dissatisfaction he is experiencing. The maximization principle would hold even if the person were choosing between two different ways of being executed.

Given this understanding of maximization, the question is what dissatisfaction (losses, negative utilities) may accrue to the individual as a result of the processes we have described thus far. There are several that especially deserve our attention.

1. The need for novelty. Mention was made earlier (pp. 14-15) of a rapidly growing literature indicating that animals, as well as man, possess an innate need for novelty. Some investigators have called it an exploratory drive, others a curiosity drive. It has been shown that reducing stimulation to a minimum (stimulus deprivation) is noxious if not utterly intolerable for people. Children also have a basic preference for complex visual displays as opposed to simple ones. These facts and many others all support the central contention.

One quickly sees, however, that the solidification of norms within a relationship could, over time, operate in a way similar to sensory deprivation. If the other person always behaves in the same way, the sheer repetition of his behavior may ultimately prove noxious. The common term for this reaction is boredom. Boredom, then, becomes a by-product of norms, and enters into the cost side of the ledger.

Unfortunately, boredom is not a cost that is often present when the norms are formed. Thus, the high level of payoffs leading to rapid norm formation may slowly be reduced once the relationship has stabilized. A prime example is marriage. In the initial stages of the relationship there may be abundant novelty. At the same time, the strong desire for maintaining the status quo may cause the partners to set up safeguards against deviation. As time goes on, deficits begin to develop as the need for novel stimulation is thwarted. A successful marriage, then, may require the maintenance of a delicate balance between fulfilling the need for norms and avoiding the stultification of the ordinary. As Erikson (1968) has put it, "Fidelity without a sense of diversity can become an obsession and a bore; diversity without a sense of fidelity, an empty relativism."

There is an important conceptual point at stake here as well. What we have said about a need for novelty contradicts what we have said about the need for consistency (pp. 73-74). If we posit a need for consistency or predictability, can we then turn around and talk in terms of a need for unpredictability or novelty? Is it legitimate to assume the existence of two diametrically opposed needs? The answer to this question on a theoretical level must be "yes." There is no reason to suppose that all needs operate

need both
consulting + unpred).
bec. man need

toward the same ends. The more common state, in fact, seems to be one of need conflict. We must be quite prepared, in building our theory, to deal with contradictory needs—and at the same time, with behavior that may fulfill some needs and thwart others at the same instant. The major problem is to understand how persons deal with such conflicts over time.

2. Norms and the individual. We have conjectured that social norms tend to maximize payoffs for the majority of any group. When we speak of cultural norms we are thus talking about maximization within the broadest segment of society. Conformity to these norms is often a legal matter. But all persons do not share the same needs, and for many the norms that exist may exact a much higher penalty. The costs for norm conformity may be at an extreme. Within small groups of people, the problem is not quite so devastating. Withdrawal from the small group is usually possible. A person can move from one group of friends to another, drop out of a fraternity, shift jobs, and so on.

However, within society at large, dropping out or shifting is an imposing proposition. In such cases either one of two results normally occurs. Either there is a symbolic if not literal "dropping out," where the person seeks niches or subcultural pockets that allow him to escape the more general norms of society. Mental institutions, organized crime, "gay" bars, and for some the academic life, may serve this function to an extent. On the other hand, the person can attempt to alter the norms—change the payoff matrix within society. The violent reaction to the Vietnam war and the multipronged attempts to alter the social and economic state of the American Negro, are cases in point. If a utopian society could ever be developed, serious thought should be given to ways of differentiating norms in such a way that the specific needs of individuals may be accommodated.

3. The crystallization of inequities. Relationships involving persons having differential amounts of power almost always contain inequities in outcomes. For the person low in power, maximization usually means settling for a lesser satisfaction than his high-power associate obtains. (There may be exceptions to this rule, in which the high-power person for some reason *allows* the low to exceed his own level of satisfaction. In fact, New Testament religion demands that the devout sacrifice their own satisfaction to benefit the needy. In this way they may opt for a higher payoff in a game where the Deity is the partner.) The development and solidification of norms may seal the fate of the low-power person for long periods of time. As the norms become sanctified and ritualized, inequity on an objective level comes to be viewed as equitable. Over time, the tribute paid to a king becomes an obligation that seems right and just in the eyes of the populace. Vestiges of this sentiment still remain in several industrial countries where kings with virtually no power continue to live in wealth, and the majority of the population is only too willing to contribute permanently to their support.

Much the same condition has existed in the United States with respect to the Negro minority. The inequities crystallized by the institution of slavery became sanctified, and over time, the impoverished condition of the Negroes came to be viewed as appropriate, by both whites and Negroes alike. It has taken a good many years to alter this pattern, and if it were not for the extensive campaign to develop a new set of learned needs (carried on by government leaders and Black Nationalists alike), little change would have been wrought. We shall continue our discussion of this issue in a moment.

4. Norms within a changing environment. Once a set of norms has become crystallized and inflexible, the stage may be set for grave problems. These are problems largely due to external sources. In the first place, the outside environment may change in such a way that if the participants in a relationship continue their pattern of behavior, they will receive negative payoffs. Many social institutions, where the norms have become formalized, furnish good examples. Such groups continuously face the threat of becoming obsolete in a constantly changing environment. A commitment to a set of stabilized norms, then, causes the institution to be less capable of adapting. One need only witness the problems within the Catholic Church in adapting to the grave reality of the population explosion, or within the railroad industry as air transportation has developed, to appreciate the proportions of this difficulty.

Additional problems are created when external sources provide *one* of the members with an increased amount of power or cause him to develop new and different needs. If crystallization of norms has created barriers to change, the result may be severe. The participant with the increased power or different needs must exercise his power even more strongly or demonstrate his needs even more expressly. This additional pressure is required because of the resistance of the norm. The racial situation in the United States well illustrates these points. Not only has the Negro experienced an increase in power (largely through legal support), but his needs are no longer what they were even a decade or two ago. And yet, even with the backing of the Supreme Court and congressional legislation, actual change in behavioral patterns has been slow in developing. The increased needs for objective equality and the rights of full citizenship have been thwarted by the inertia of long-standing norms. More recent forms of extremist activity—riots, burning, looting, and so on—might well have been anticipated.

In facing some of the problems that norms create, we have also set the stage for the discussion in the next chapter. Here we shall deal with ways in which people deviously increase their rewards without altering the system.

REFERENCES

Adams, J. S., Inequity in social exchange, in *Advances in Experimental Social Psychology* (L. Berkowitz, ed.), Vol. II. New York: Academic Press, 1965.

Adams, J. S., and Patricia R. Jacobson, Effects of wage inequities on work quality. *Journal of Abnormal and Social Psychology*, **69**, 19-25, 1964.

Biddle, B. J., and E. J. Thomas, *Role Theory*. New York: John Wiley and Sons, 1966.

Brehm, J. W., and A. R. Cohen, *Explorations in Cognitive Dissonance*. New York: John Wiley and Sons, 1962.

Clark, J. V., A preliminary investigation of some unconscious assumptions affecting labor efficiency in eight supermarkets. Unpublished doctoral dissertation, Graduate School of Business Administration, Harvard University, 1958.

Erikson, E. H., *Identity, Youth and Crisis*. New York: W. W. Norton, 1968.

Festinger, L., *A Theory of Cognitive Dissonance*. Evanston: Row, Peterson, 1957.

Fowler, H., *Curiosity and Exploratory Behavior*. New York: Macmillan, 1965.

Gergen, K. J., Phoebe Diebold, M. Seipel, and Christine Gresser, Obligation, resource differences, and reactions to beneficent actions. In preparation.

Goffman, E., *Behavior in Public Places*. New York: Free Press of Glencoe, 1963.

Gouldner, A. W., The norm of reciprocity: a preliminary statement. *American Sociological Review*, **25**, 161-179, 1960.

Hollander, E. P., Competence and conformity in the acceptance of influence. *Journal of Abnormal and Social Psychology*, **61**, 365-369, 1960.

Hollander, E. P., Conformity, status and idiosyncrasy credit. *Psychological Review*, **65**, 117-127, 1958.

Hollander, E. P., *Leaders, Groups and Influence*. New York: Oxford University Press, 1964.

Homans, G. C., Social behavior as exchange. *American Journal of Sociology*, **63**, 597-606, 1958.

Homans, G. C., *Social Behavior: Its Elementary Forms*. New York: Harcourt, Brace, 1961.

Jennings, Helen Hall, *Leadership and Isolation*. New York: Longmans, Green, 1950.

Kiesler, C. A., and Sara B. Kiesler, *Conformity*. Reading, Mass.: Addison-Wesley, 1969.

Leavitt, H. J., Some effects of certain communication patterns on group performance. *Journal of Abnormal and Social Psychology,* **56**, 38-50, 1951.

Mann, R. D., A review of the relationships between personality and performance in small groups. *Psychological Bulletin,* **56**, 241-270, 1959.

Simmel, G., *The Sociology of Georg Simmel* (K. H. Wolff, ed. and transl.). Glencoe, Ill.: Free Press, 1950.

Thibaut, J. W., and H. H. Kelley, *The Social Psychology of Groups.* New York: John Wiley and Sons, 1959.

Zimbardo, P. G., and E. B. Ebbesen, *Influencing Attitudes and Changing Behavior.* Reading, Mass.: Addison-Wesley, 1969.

CHAPTER SEVEN

The Tactical Manipulation of Outcomes

It might seem thus far that an individual's lot is determined for him at the very outset of a relationship. By taking a good look at the norms as they exist around him, he can obtain a fairly accurate picture of what he may expect. After all, a person can usually estimate what his level of enjoyment will be in those various groups available to him. You know roughly what you may expect by spending an evening with your parents, as opposed to cronies of the same sex, or a friend of the opposite sex, and so on. In each of these relationships, norms already exist in one form or another. And if they haven't developed, in most instances the "new" relationship will follow the established pattern for the culture at large. In spite of all the spontaneity one experiences in a new relationship, the pattern of that relationship is more or less predetermined at the outset. Certain behaviors are excluded, others a necessity.

And yet, even within the limits set by social norms, seldom are one's outcomes completely immutable, incapable of being altered. We have characterized the human being as a creature of *maximization*. That is, he can be counted on to search continuously for ways of increasing his rewards at less and less cost to himself. To be sure, norms have a way of dividing rewards and costs among persons on a predictable basis; the reciprocity norm even makes it clear that rewards and costs should be roughly equalized (consideration of power differences notwithstanding). But unless norms are major sources of satisfaction for the person, he can be counted on to find alternative if not devious ways of obtaining greater rewards at less cost.

In general, people look at this maximization "in spite of the norms" in a dim light. After all, we are pointing here to ways in which people calculate their payoffs, assess their surroundings, and set about manipulating the situation to their benefit, quite often at the expense of others. In terms of the reciprocity norm, we are speaking of ways in which people obtain more than their "fair share."

It is interesting in this respect to look at social relationships as a type of battlefield. Each participant wants a victory in terms of as much gratification as he can receive. However, if everyone set out in an uninhibited and straightforward way to achieve these ends, most would perish. Complete anarchy threatens everyone with loss. Thus, norms and rules are developed to maintain and support the social order. These norms exact a toll from each participant, but typically provide a satisfactory level of outcomes for the majority. However, at the same time, the norms and laws can be looked upon as the documented strategy of the potential enemy. The problem for the individual, then, is to calculate ways of gaining as much as possible for himself without destroying the laws or norms that furnish protection.

This, of course, is a very grim picture of the human state. Few people would agree that their behavior is based on such premises. In truth, *all* behavior is not. For most people, the socialization process has instilled a loathing for such manipulative behavior. People receive psychological payoffs for obeying the reciprocity norm, for example. And even when one's behavior does have a manipulative coloration, the instigator might be the last to recognize or admit it. Recognition would bring personal dissatisfaction; admission could incur social censure.

If there are strong sanctions against such behavior, and people avoid recognizing it in themselves or admitting it to others, how can it be studied? The pitfalls are indeed formidable, and basic problems are only beginning to be solved. However, the logic supporting the existence of such behavior is so compelling, and the behavior in question so interesting, that psychologists have pushed forward where angels fear to tread.

The present chapter will sample from research in this general problem area. First, however, it is useful to distinguish between two major forms that the tactical manipulation of outcomes may take. When one stops to think about them, one realizes that we have all engaged in these behaviors at one time or another.

1. Increase through other's loss. There are a number of ways in which a person may increase his own payoffs at the expense of another. Such tactics become manipulative, in the present sense, when (1) the individual shields the knowledge of his increased payoffs from the other person in the relationship, or (2) the other is prevented from knowing that he is the loser. If the increment in satisfaction is exposed, then by virtue of the reciprocity norm, the other member of the relationship has a right to expect his own positive outcomes to be increased—an expectation that would most likely *cost* self. By the same token, if the other's outcomes are reduced as a result of one's own increase in satisfaction, the other would have the right to exact retribution, also at cost to self.

Examples of manipulative increases in satisfaction might include the secretary's prolonged coffee break about which her employer remains unaware. She gains in pleasure; her boss loses her time without knowledge. Or the caller who has been kept waiting may solicit apologies for his "suffering." At the same time, he has found something extremely rewarding to do in the meantime (e.g., making a date with the secretary of the man who has kept him waiting—undoubtedly the secretary on the prolonged coffee break). In both cases the individuals are taking advantage of the normative distribution of outcomes, increasing their own satisfaction at a cost not recognized by the other.

2. Increase through other's satisfaction. One also stands to gain when he provides the other with increased satisfaction at no or low cost to himself. In this way he may take advantage of the reciprocity norm, and oblige the other to increase his positive outcomes in return for the benefit he *seems* to have provided. This conduct becomes "illegitimate" when the person makes it appear that the rewards the other is receiving have been at cost to self. Newlyweds often take advantage of this situation. They may have an attic full of unwanted wedding gifts that they bestow on others. The receivers, however, feel the gifts were costly to the newlyweds and are thus the more obligated to return a favor.

The major contribution to understanding in this general area has been made by Edward E. Jones (1964) in his analysis of ingratiation. This work elucidates the ways in which a person manipulates others into feeling that he, the manipulator, is attractive or deserving of rewards. Among other things, Jones's research has established conditions under which people will flatter others, or conform to their opinions—giving satisfaction at no cost to themselves—primarily in order to gain more for themselves. Flattery can be an especially useful technique. For one thing, it plays heavily on the reciprocity norm. If one has complimented or praised you, the feeling of obligation to return the favor can be very strong. The Don Juan knows this well. In addition, flattery causes the victim to feel more positive about himself. As we pointed out earlier (p. 46), this pleasure or self-satisfaction is at the heart of social attraction. And those who are attracted to others are prone to do good things for them.

Having glimpsed two major strategies of manipulation, we are in a better position to ask how one goes about researching such issues. And if they can be researched, what generalizations can be developed? In the remainder of this chapter we shall first look at a single investigation which attempts to demonstrate such strategies of manipulation at work. Then we shall consider the intriguing problems of individual differences in the proclivity to manipulate—what kind of person is most likely to engage in such activities?

INCREASING REWARDS THROUGH INGRATIATION

Of the two tactical manipulations described above, the no-cost increase in the other's satisfaction has received the greater attention in the laboratory. This experimentation has been conducted largely by Jones and his colleagues. One of their particular interests grew out of the widespread concern in our society with behavior in status hierarchies. "Pecking orders" prevail throughout society, on both the human and the animal level. As unfortunate as it may be, one's value as a human being within society is often equated with his rank in such hierarchies. Seniority is sainthood and it's the little man "what gets the rot." So "important" are the problems that the young man of today confronts that even our leisure hours may be filled with the drama of the situation, from "How to Succeed in Business Without Really Trying" to "Room at the Top." Like Greek drama, such fare is cathartic; it blows off collective steam.

Life for the low-power person in a hierarchy presents special problems. The norms usually provide him with an inferior level of outcomes, and if the hierarchy happens to be a formal organization (e.g., industrial or military), the hurdles in his way forward are carefully monitored. In essence, he has little and it is difficult to achieve more than a meager gain through normal channels. In addition, the high-power person is able to bestow rewards of great magnitude. And to incur his disfavor may bring great misfortune down upon one. Thus, the high-power person becomes a prime target for ingratiation attempts by subordinates.

An investigation by Jones, Gergen, Gumpert, and Thibaut (1965) was particularly concerned with the plight of the man who finds himself "behind the eight ball"—faced with a task for which his capacities are ill suited, and yet for which his performance will be evaluated by his superior. Placed in such a position, it was felt that the individual will strive with every means available to improve his lot, whether legitimately or not.

It was first hoped to demonstrate that ingratiation tactics depend largely on whether the formal structure leaves the high-power person open to manipulation. You might consider, for example, the difference between an organization in which performance is assessed uniformly by a machine and one in which personal judgment prevails. In the former instance, there may be little to gain through ingratiating oneself with superiors; in the latter case, one might use friendship to influence performance evaluation. In terms of the original matrix formulation (Chapter Three), this would be to provide the powerful person with positive outcomes in one area (where the personal cost is little) in order to gain positive outcomes for self in a second area—a trade of "friendship" for good ratings on performance. It was thus predicted that the tendency to establish such a trade would be more likely when the system left the high-status individual open to social influence.

The second aim of the study was to explore whether the personal characteristics of the high-power evaluator influence the ingratiation tactics chosen for use. You will recall from our discussion on interpersonal bargaining that the identity of the other person was an important factor in predicting exploitation (see pp. 59-61). In the same way, certain kinds of persons might be seen as "pushovers" for one type of ingratiation tactic, while others much less so. The personal characteristics of interest in this study are captured by the widely observed stereotype of the "hard-nosed" versus the "soft-nosed" boss—the former advocating efficiency, productivity, and respect, and the latter valuing "togetherness" and affability in getting the job done. So common and persistent are these patterns that one might almost think they were genetically determined.

The two ingratiation tactics of present concern were those of opinion conformity and self-presentation. Agreement with another's opinions is a common method of providing him satisfaction. Not only does it signify approval of the other's thinking and behavior, but it may remove doubt (decrease dissonance) or increase his feelings of clarity on an issue. One may also select certain ways of presenting or describing himself to the other. Self-presentation may be used to make oneself appear more attractive. In a status hierarchy, having attractive characteristics causes one to be more valued as part of the organization. Being attractive also causes one's social support to be more highly valued.

In order to assess the effects of the person's openness to influence and his individual characteristics on ingratiation tactics, undergraduates worked on a task for which they could earn up to $10 for a superior performance. The task was to judge the potential effectiveness of advertising slogans in selling various products (e.g., neckties, washing machines, and skin cream). In a practice session, it also became clear to each subject that he was not very good at the job—decidedly inferior to others who had participated in the task. At the same time that he was confronted with the threat of poor performance, he was faced with one of the following external conditions.

Half the subjects in the experiment found that the task evaluator, purported to be a graduate student in the School of Business Administration, was allowed autonomy in making his evaluation. Subjects were led to believe that the graduate student would use his own discretion in deciding whether the slogan choices were good ones or not. In effect, the system left him potentially open to influence (Open Judgment condition). The other half of the subjects found the structure of the situation did not permit the supervisor to exercise any discretionary power. His decisions as to what the correct answers were had already been recorded, and judgments of performance were thus fixed (Closed Judgment condition).

The second major variation was in the personal characteristics of the superior. In order to execute this variation, the full task was said to involve the task worker (the subject) and his superior in a full interchange of information about themselves, much like a normal working relationship in a business. As part of this procedure, the workers would first be allowed to listen to the superior answer questions concerning his views on various topics. Half the subjects in each of the above conditions subsequently heard the superior respond to questions from the experimenter in a way that emphasized the hard-nosed productivity orientation. He stressed the quality and quantity of job performance above all else. Talent and perseverance were those qualities he valued most in a worker (Productivity condition). The remaining subjects heard quite a different set of opinions, ones that emphasized social solidarity. In this instance the supervisor was heard to value the "human" side of business, and to stress the spirit of cooperation and the importance of getting along with others (Solidarity condition).

Once the stage was set for each of the four conditions, it was possible to measure the effects on opinion conformity and self-presentation. In the former case, subjects were exposed to the supervisor's opinions on various aspects of student life. Opinion conformity was assessed by how much the subject would *change* his true opinions (as measured some weeks before the study) to agree with the supervisor's. The self-presentation measure consisted of a series of attribute dimensions along which the subject rated himself. The attributes reflected either productivity (e.g., efficient-ineffi-

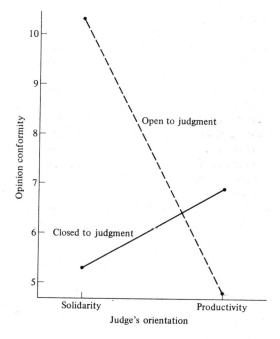

Fig. 7.1 Conformity as an ingratiation tactic. (Adapted from Jones, Gergen, Gumpert, and Thibaut, 1965.)

cient) or social solidarity (e.g., friendly-aloof), and all self-ratings were to be communicated to the supervisor.

What were the effects of the various stimulus conditions on conformity and self-presentation? Figure 7.1 shows the major results for opinion conformity in the four conditions. It is quickly noticeable that there is one and only one condition in which conformity is singled out and used as an ingratiation tactic: the Open Judgment-Solidarity condition. The remainder of the means form a statistically undifferentiated cluster. When the supervisor is seen as a "nice guy" who values affability and getting along with others, and when the system leaves such a man open to making judgments, the task worker leaps to the breach. He forgoes his honest opinion, and alters it to agree with his supervisor.

Why does one not find more conformity in the Open Judgment-Productivity condition? After all, the supervisor in this condition did have freedom to bestow rewards. Although we cannot be certain, there is good reason to believe that subjects, seeing the supervisor as "tough-minded" and opposed to the "wishy-washy," avoided this tactic of improving their outcomes.

When we turn to the tactic of self-presentation, we find a very different pattern of results. The most important analysis for our purposes was of the tendency to describe oneself positively on productivity dimensions as opposed to solidarity dimensions. By subtracting self-rating scores on one set of dimensions from the other, a single *productivity emphasis* score could be derived. Here it was found that the subjects' display of themselves as "efficient," "intelligent," and so on was most pronounced in the Open Judgment-Productivity condition. When the supervisor is free to make decisions and is seen as productivity oriented, then his subordinates begin to modify their public image. Specifically, they cause themselves to be seen in a very positive light on traits that would be most appreciated by the supervisor.

In summary, opinion conformity and self-presentation may both be used to secure better outcomes from a superior. The extent to which they are used may depend on a number of factors. Specifically, conformity is used most when a "soft" supervisor is in a position to make his own decisions. The tactic of inflating one's public image, on the other hand, seems to be most often used when the "efficiency expert" is in a similar position.

Thus far we have seen that situational factors may play a crucial role in determining when, where, and how much tactical manipulation may occur in a relationship. However, as you scan the social environment, you are also aware that there are some people who seem to engage in much more of this type of behavior than others—who seem much more bent on getting ahead "without really trying." Several psychologists have shared in this observation, and the results of their work provide a valuable adjunct to the account we have given thus far.

THE MACHIAVELLIAN APPROACH TO HUMAN RELATIONS

The study of individual differences in the tendency to manipulate began almost accidentally. Christie and Merton (1958) were investigating the effects of medical school experience on medical students. They were particularly interested in the possible effects of a medical education on values and attitudes of the students. One of their major discoveries was that medical students changed markedly in their view of people. Over the years they came to see others as impersonal objects, not particularly trustworthy, and open to manipulation should this be necessary to achieve one's ends. Possibly the students were beginning to see the world more realistically? However, Christie and Merton felt that the most adequate way of describing this syndrome of changes was to use the term Machiavellianism.

Christie and Geis subsequently set out to construct a measure that would reflect this dimension more directly. The measure which they developed consisted of a series of 20 value statements, to which respondents indicated their degree of agreement or disagreement. Many of the statements directly reflected sentiments expressed by Machiavelli in *The Prince*. For example, people were asked whether they agreed with the following:

1. The best way to handle people is to tell them what they want to hear.

2. Anyone who completely trusts anyone else is asking for trouble.

3. One should take action only when sure it is morally right.

4. All in all, it is better to be humble and honest than to be important and dishonest.

People who tended to agree with the first two statements and disagree with the second pair would be given a higher score in Machiavellian propensities.

Early work with the scale did show that responses to the items tended to cohere. That is, if an individual tended to agree strongly with one Machiavellian statement, he would also tend more often than not to agree with the others. Scores on the test were also found to be highly reliable over time. The next important question was whether scores on the measure could be used to predict actual behavior. Were these value statements indicative of how the person would treat other human beings?

Perhaps the most convincing evidence for the validity of the test came from a study (Geis, Christie, and Nelson, 1963) in which each subject was asked to perform the role of an experimenter whose task was to administer an important personality test to another subject. He was told that for experimental purposes it would be desirable if he could distract the test taker from his work. The subject was told that he might confuse or distract the test taker in any way he wished. In effect, the subjects were placed in a position in which they were at complete liberty to manipulate another person. They were given an opportunity to show initiative, to fulfill the experimenter's request as little or as much as they liked and in whatever way they desired. The question was whether people who showed high agreement with the items on the test would be more manipulative than those who tended to disagree with the Machiavellian statements.

The behavior of the subjects was observed and recorded from a position behind a one-way mirror. The results were striking. High scorers on the Machiavellian test found twice as many different ways to manipulate the test taker than did low scorers. Not only did they think of more ways to inflict misery, but they manipulated him more than twice as often.

These statistically reliable findings hardly capture the imaginative zeal with which the high scorers went about their work. Geis's (1965) description of the actions of one high scorer nicely fills the void:

> The list of manipulations performed by one high includes, among other things: rubs hands together in the stereotyped gesture of eager anticipation; bends over double, unties shoe, shakes foot, reties shoe; jingles contents of pocket noisily, pulls out chapstick and applies it while staring absent-mindedly at ceiling; whistles; slaps leg and straightens up noisily and abruptly in chair; taps pencil rhythmically on table; hums; reaches around table divider and carefully knocks it over (this produces a loud crash and sends papers on table flying in all directions); after ten-second dead silence apologizes profusely to test-taker for "distracting" him; erases vigorously on blank margin of test-taker's score sheet (divider board prevents him from seeing that all of his scores are not being erased); comments, with serious frown at one-way vision mirror, "I feel like I'm on TV, don't you?" (followed by delighted, "confiding" grin at mirror as soon as test-taker returns his attention to test booklet); holds match book in both hands above divider board in full view of test-taker, tears out matches one by one, dropping each into ash tray; tears up empty matchbook cover and drops pieces ostentatiously into ash tray; dismantles own ballpoint pen behind divider board, uses spring to shoot it, parts flying across the room; jumps from chair, dashes across room to retrieve pen parts saying, "Sorry, I'm a little nervous."

Additional research has shown that high scorers on the Machiavellian scale, in contrast to low, tend to be more aggressive in game behavior, better at "conning" others to gain outcomes for themselves, and more likely to achieve better grades in large lecture courses (intelligence held constant). To their own chagrin, social psychologists tend to have high scores on the measure.

However, the next step, and an exceedingly important one, will be to assess the antecedents of Machiavellianism. What sort of environment is apt to engender this proclivity? Is the tendency generally developed early in life; or, like the medical student, do people learn to become Machiavellian as they are thrown to the wolves of the workday world?

REFERENCES

Blau, P., *Exchange and Power in Social Life*. New York: John Wiley and Sons, 1964.

Christie, R., and Florence Geis, *Studies in Machiavellianism*. New York: Academic Press, in press.

Christie, R., and R. K. Merton, Procedures for the sociological study of the values climate of medical schools. *Journal of Medical Education*, **33**, 125-153, 1958.

Geis, Florence, Machiavellianism and the manipulation of one's fellow men. Paper presented at the 1965 meeting of the American Psychological Association.

Geis, Florence, R. Christie, and C. Nelson, In search of the Machiavel. Mimeographed, Columbia University, 1963.

Goffman, E., *Interaction Ritual*. New York: Doubleday Anchor, 1967.

Goffman, E., *The Presentation of Self in Everyday Life*. New York: Doubleday Anchor, 1959.

Jones, E. E., *Ingratiation: A Social Psychological Analysis*. New York: Appleton-Century-Crofts, 1964.

Jones, E. E., K. J. Gergen, P. Gumpert, and J. W. Thibaut, Some conditions affecting the use of ingratiation to influence performance evaluation. *Journal of Personality and Social Psychology*, **1**, 613-625, 1965.

Ludwig, A. M., *The Importance of Lying*. Springfield, Ill.: Charles C. Thomas, 1965.

McCall, G. J., and J. L. Simmons, *Identities and Interactions*. New York: Free Press, 1966.

CHAPTER EIGHT

Failure and Further

In all too few pages an attempt has been made to lay a foundation for a theory of social interaction. The orientation has been a biased one, drawing heavily from a growing tradition to which the rough label "behavioral exchange" has been applied. But now that we have laid out the essentials, we might step back and take a critical look at our handiwork. Where are the major flaws? What, if anything, could be done to correct these difficulties? Where must the future take us if the exchange orientation is to remain viable? This chapter will deal with four such issues.

1. The vicissitudes of motivation. In Chapters Two and Three we dealt with the concept of satisfaction and more particularly with the problem of when a satisfier is not satisfying. As you may recall, it was shown that deprivation or satiation within a situation would affect the value of a class of satisfiers. When deprived, the satisfier becomes more valuable to the person. Second, it was stressed that as a result of their earlier training, certain people are more highly motivated than others to obtain certain kinds of satisfaction (viz., social approval). If anything, the research examples provided in these chapters presented an optimistic picture. They affirmed the capacity of behavioral science to account for the shifts that might take place in the value of satisfiers over time.

This optimism is misleading, and for a number of reasons. First, our early examples were drawn primarily from the literature on social approval. But consider for a moment the number of motives or types of satisfaction relevant to an individual. Not only are there the biological drives, but, as we noted in Chapter Two, there might be a large number of learned motives. In fact, the number of learned motives could be considered infinite. Any type of behavior associated with or instrumental to achieving pleasure could come to have satisfaction value. Kinsey's research on sex behavior, for example, shows that the number of different activities providing human beings with sexual gratification is enormous. From a theoretical viewpoint, almost any behavior associated with or instrumental to obtaining sexual satisfaction could develop a capacity to motivate behavior.

Second, once we realize the magnitude of the number of potential motives, we must also recognize that any number of them may be competing for dominance in any given situation. At any moment there are a wide number of activities that might give a person pleasure. Some way of predicting which motives will be *prepotent*, that is, most likely to influence behavior at the moment, must be developed. Maslow (1954) has spoken of *hierarchies of needs,* in which certain motives must be fulfilled prior to motives of lesser strength. However, any simple notion of hierarchies will hardly suffice when it is recalled that the motive state may fluctuate from moment to moment, and that any given behavior may satisfy or thwart several different motives simultaneously.

The problems are compounded when it is further realized that the multiple motives operating for different individuals at different times may also change with the history of the culture. A strong case was made in Chapter Three for the importance of approval motivation. But approval seeking is relevant to the present generation alone, and a century from now people may be less concerned about the approval of others. Perhaps people of the next century will derive major satisfaction from knowledge about other lands or planets, or from finding a small plot of soil that has not been contaminated by radioactive fallout.

A further problem follows from this argument. If the strength of learned motives varies over the years, as it most certainly does, can the theoretical principles relevant to one of these motives be generalized to others? Are the principles currently being developed about the operation of approval motivation useful in dealing with motives for power, aggression, tranquillity, and so on? Is a new theory required for each type of motivation? In answer to this question, perhaps the most that can be hoped for is that at some very abstract level there may be a similarity in the operation of all learned motives. All, for example, may be subject to arousal within a given situation, depending on the stimulus present. And the value of a given amount of reinforcement may be reduced when it is constantly provided. But these are broad statements indeed. In dealing with the more detailed aspects of these motives, such as specifying the effective stimuli that will arouse them, tracing the correlates in the autonomic nervous system, knowing how each motive operates in relation to other motives, and so on, much less in the way of generality might be expected.

We have said, then, that the number of learned motives is near infinite, that such motives vary in strength from moment to moment and through history, and that there may be difficulties in developing principles that apply to all. Are these insurmountable obstacles? Perhaps we betray too much of the traditional optimism of American culture in answering "no."

But it is very clear that major work on both a theoretical and an empirical level remains to be done on the problem of multiple and shifting motives.

2. The place of cognition. It was made clear in the initial chapter that the exchange orientation was heavily empirical. It has been cautious about utilizing concepts referring to mental processes. And yet, in spite of our efforts, we have found it necessary to utilize a good number of hypothetical constructs. Certain of these constructs lead us to the borderline between exchange theory and a second venerable tradition in psychology, the cognitive orientation.

Cognitive theorists have played a key role in the history of psychology since the days of Wundt and the German introspectionists. In social psychology this tradition flowered most prosperously in the 1940's with Kurt Lewin's ground-breaking theories. Since Lewin's time, several different branches have sprouted. One of these, and most germane to our purposes, has centered on processes that bias the individual's understanding and evaluation of the world. Many such processes are discussed in another contribution to this series (Hastorf and Polefka, 1969); others are discussed as they relate to social influence (Zimbardo, 1969) and social attraction (Berscheid and Walster, 1969). Research in this area highlights a number of factors causing the person to misjudge the world about him, label his emotional states in arbitrary ways, rationalize the value of outcomes, and so on.

Our discussion of hidden assumptions at the close of Chapter Four also led us to the threshold of this tradition. It seems clear that the next step, and a painful one for many, is to cross this threshold in resolute fashion. Why? Because of several major problems that must ultimately be overcome if the exchange orientation is to continue to flourish. These problems include:

a) How individuals assign values to various outcomes. We have already noted how the satisfaction derived from a given activity may shift from moment to moment. Cognitive theory may be essential in helping us to understand the laws by which these shifts take place. If people assign greater value to outcomes to which they have devoted great effort, a concept such as *cognitive dissonance* (cf. Festinger, 1957; Zimbardo, 1969) may be required. When we find that motivation increases when there is a high probability of gratification, we may need to add concepts having to do with probability estimates (cf. Atkinson and Feather, 1966). And if descriptions and evaluations of self are important predictors of behavior, a notion such as self-conception (cf. Gordon and Gergen, 1968) proves highly useful.

b) How persons decide among competing alternatives. Even if we could pinpoint the processes by which people determine the utility of outcomes, the crucial problem would remain of how they reach solutions in the face of competing alternatives. The research on interpersonal bargaining (Chapter Five) brought this problem to the fore most clearly. True, it was found that bargaining behavior could be modified systematically as a result of varying conditions. But such attempts were only a crude beginning.

In what appears to be a simple context, such as that of bargaining experimentation, people may consider a broad number of factors simultaneously. They might consider the probability that the other would exploit them if they were cooperative, the degree to which they value cooperation, the possibility that they would feel guilty if they engaged in exploitation, their need for the money involved, ways in which they might signal the other to cooperate, the chances of their facing the other after the bargaining, and the itch on their big toe. Exactly how, out of the welter of information with which the individual is deluged, he reaches a decision as to the *one* appropriate behavior is beyond our understanding at this point. To solve this problem, we shall undoubtedly have to deal in terms of thought processes and decision making.

3. General psychology or the psychology of college students? Our third major problem is less formidable, but highly important. You have no doubt been struck by the number of psychological studies in which college students have served as subjects. Inasmuch as most behavioral science is conducted by investigators whose primary role (at least on paper) is college teaching, this fact is hardly surprising. However, the continued and exclusive use of college students in such research is fraught with risk.

Exchange theory, like other theories of behavior, purports to be highly general. That is, the theorist more or less assumes that principles of social behavior, once supported by empirical results, are highly general in nature. He may assume that such principles might aid in predicting the behavior of people in all walks of life. And yet, when one considers the peculiar population on which such principles are based, this assumption becomes problematic. College students are hardly a random sample of the general population. They face unfamiliar problems that they never again will encounter; profound changes in the bodily state are taking place; they exist in a unique and highly pressurized environment. They are a rare and motley species at best. Is it safe to base general theories on data emanating from such a group? True, these theories may be very accurate in making predictions. But the final result may be a complete psychology of the late adolescent.

4. Science or history? The final issue is broader in nature, and relevant not only to exchange theory but to all scientific treatments of social interaction. The common premise underlying the scientific analysis of social behavior is that knowledge is *cumulative*. More specifically, knowledge in the behavioral sciences is assumed to accumulate in the same fashion as in the physical sciences. This is, first, to assume that facts remain stable—that the rate of falling bodies is the same in the year 1500 as it is in 1900; or the greater the amount of reinforcement for a given behavior, the greater the likelihood of the behavior's recurrence, regardless of when that relationship is tested. Second, it is to assume that the more facts gathered, the more powerful will be the resulting theoretical statement.

If these assumptions were not valid, the study of social behavior would be historical in nature. If today's fact were not tomorrow's fact, if events were not repeatable, then each specific experiment would only be charting a set of unique historical occurrences. There would be little in the way of accumulated knowledge, because one could never depend on past events to recur. The effects of any circumstance would always have to be tested anew. Viable theory would be impossible to develop.

It may well be that behavioral science is predominantly historical as opposed to scientific, in the sense in which we have used these terms. Why? Primarily because in the behavioral sciences, as contrasted with the physical sciences, "accumulated knowledge" may affect the population about which conclusions have been drawn. On a mundane level, this means that no experimenter will allow his subjects to know his hypotheses before he tests them. Their preknowledge may bias his results. On a more global level, psychological theories of behavior impinge on large segments of the society. College courses, the newsstands, and the mass media all disseminate knowledge about psychology. These views are assimilated, stored, and may affect behavior in any situation thereafter. The reader of this book cannot remain unaffected by its contents.

By way of illustration, it has been said that social conformity can never be studied in the same way now as it was a decade ago, and precisely because of the widespread public attention that psychologists have brought to the phenomenon. People evaluate conformity more negatively, are more sensitized to conformity pressures, and indeed, may counter-conform where they would have conformed a decade earlier. In the same way, psychoanalytic theory may have sealed its fate by having become so widely read, and Marxian theory may have created revolution by its very existence.

The better the theory, the greater the likelihood of its influencing the culture. If exchange theory becomes highly reliable and thus widely taught, it might thereby cease to predict. It would, of course, be possible to develop and test theories about how people react to behavioral science theories. Indeed, people do seem to react to knowledge in predictable ways. But these second-order theories are subject to the same arguments that we have raised thus far. They, too, become *information* that the person takes into account in determining his actions.

Thus, both theories and the facts upon which they are grounded may have a limited life span. Theories may be accurate during short periods of history; and the more accurate, the shorter these periods. In essence, behavioral "science" is closely akin to historical description. However, this should hardly dissuade us from continuing in our systematic study of behavior. Only through the understanding of social behavior in the years preceding can we truly grasp the meaning of behavior at any given period of history.

REFERENCES

Atkinson, J. W., and N. T. Feather, *A Theory of Achievement Motivation.* New York: John Wiley and Sons, 1966.

Berscheid, Ellen, and Elaine C. Walster, *Interpersonal Attraction.* Reading, Mass.: Addison-Wesley, 1969.

Deutsch, M., Field theory in social psychology, in *The Handbook of Social Psychology* (2nd edition, G. Lindzey and E. Aronson, eds.), Vol. I. Reading, Mass.: Addison-Wesley, 1968.

Festinger, L., *A Theory of Cognitive Dissonance.* Evanston: Row, Peterson, 1957.

Gordon, C., and K. J. Gergen (eds.), *The Self in Social Interaction,* Vol. I. New York: John Wiley and Sons, 1968.

Hastorf, A., and Judith Polefka, *Person Perception.* Reading, Mass.: Addison-Wesley, 1969.

Lewin, K., *A Dynamic Theory of Personality.* New York: McGraw-Hill, 1935.

Lewin, K., *Field Theory in Social Science.* New York: Harper and Sons, 1951.

Maslow, A. H., *Motivation and Personality.* New York: Harper and Sons, 1954.

Merton, R. K., The self-fulfilling prophesy, in *Social Theory and Social Structure.* Glencoe, Ill.: Free Press, 1961.

Rosenthal, R., *Experimenter Effects in Behavioral Research.* New York: Appleton-Century-Crofts, 1966.

Zajonc, R. B., Cognitive theories in social psychology, in *The Handbook of Social Psychology* (2nd edition, G. Lindzey and E. Aronson, eds.), Vol. I. Reading, Mass.: Addison-Wesley, 1968.

Zimbardo, P. G., and E. B. Ebbesen, *Influencing Attitudes and Changing Behavior.* Reading, Mass.: Addison-Wesley, 1969.

DE79876543210